The Ancient Near East: A Very Short Introduction

VERY SHORT INTRODUCTIONS are for anyone wanting a stimulating and accessible way in to a new subject. They are written by experts and have been published in more than 25 languages worldwide.

The series began in 1995 and now represents a wide variety of topics in history, philosophy, religion, science, and the humanities. The VSI library now contains more than 300 volumes—a Very Short Introduction to everything from ancient Egypt and Indian philosophy to conceptual art and cosmology—and will continue to grow in a variety of disciplines.

Very Short Introductions available now:

ADVERTISING Winston Fletcher
AFRICAN HISTORY John Parker and Richard Rathbone
AGNOSTICISM Robin Le Poidevin
AMERICAN HISTORY Paul S. Boyer
AMERICAN IMMIGRATION David A. Gerber
AMERICAN POLITICAL PARTIES AND ELECTIONS L. Sandy Maisel
AMERICAN POLITICS Richard M. Valelly
THE AMERICAN PRESIDENCY Charles O. Jones
ANAESTHESIA Aidan O'Donnell
ANARCHISM Colin Ward
ANCIENT EGYPT Ian Shaw
ANCIENT GREECE Paul Cartledge
THE ANCIENT NEAR EAST Amanda H. Podany
ANCIENT PHILOSOPHY Julia Annas
ANCIENT WARFARE Harry Sidebottom
ANGELS David Albert Jones
ANGLICANISM Mark Chapman
THE ANGLO-SAXON AGE John Blair
THE ANIMAL KINGDOM Peter Holland
ANIMAL RIGHTS David DeGrazia
THE ANTARCTIC Klaus Dodds
ANTISEMITISM Steven Beller
ANXIETY Daniel Freeman and Jason Freeman
THE APOCRYPHAL GOSPELS Paul Foster
ARCHAEOLOGY Paul Bahn
ARCHITECTURE Andrew Ballantyne
ARISTOCRACY William Doyle
ARISTOTLE Jonathan Barnes
ART HISTORY Dana Arnold
ART THEORY Cynthia Freeland
ASTROBIOLOGY David C. Catling
ATHEISM Julian Baggini
AUGUSTINE Henry Chadwick
AUSTRALIA Kenneth Morgan
AUTISM Uta Frith
THE AVANT GARDE David Cottington
THE AZTECS Davíd Carrasco
BACTERIA Sebastian G. B. Amyes
BARTHES Jonathan Culler
THE BEATS David Sterritt
BEAUTY Roger Scruton
BESTSELLERS John Sutherland

THE BIBLE John Riches
BIBLICAL ARCHAEOLOGY Eric H. Cline
BIOGRAPHY Hermione Lee
THE BLUES Elijah Wald
THE BOOK OF MORMON Terryl Givens
BORDERS Alexander C. Diener and Joshua Hagen
THE BRAIN Michael O'Shea
THE BRITISH CONSTITUTION Martin Loughlin
THE BRITISH EMPIRE Ashley Jackson
BRITISH POLITICS Anthony Wright
BUDDHA Michael Carrithers
BUDDHISM Damien Keown
BUDDHIST ETHICS Damien Keown
CANCER Nicholas James
CAPITALISM James Fulcher
CATHOLICISM Gerald O'Collins
CAUSATION Stephen Mumford and Rani Lill Anjum
THE CELL Terence Allen and Graham Cowling
THE CELTS Barry Cunliffe
CHAOS Leonard Smith
CHILDREN'S LITERATURE Kimberley Reynolds
CHINESE LITERATURE Sabina Knight
CHOICE THEORY Michael Allingham
CHRISTIAN ART Beth Williamson
CHRISTIAN ETHICS D. Stephen Long
CHRISTIANITY Linda Woodhead
CITIZENSHIP Richard Bellamy
CIVIL ENGINEERING David Muir Wood
CLASSICAL MYTHOLOGY Helen Morales
CLASSICS Mary Beard and John Henderson
CLAUSEWITZ Michael Howard
CLIMATE Mark Maslin
THE COLD WAR Robert McMahon
COLONIAL AMERICA Alan Taylor
COLONIAL LATIN AMERICAN LITERATURE Rolena Adorno
COMEDY Matthew Bevis
COMMUNISM Leslie Holmes
THE COMPUTER Darrel Ince
THE CONQUISTADORS Matthew Restall and Felipe Fernández-Armesto
CONSCIENCE Paul Strohm
CONSCIOUSNESS Susan Blackmore
CONTEMPORARY ART Julian Stallabrass
CONTEMPORARY FICTION Robert Eaglestone
CONTINENTAL PHILOSOPHY Simon Critchley
COSMOLOGY Peter Coles
CRITICAL THEORY Stephen Eric Bronner
THE CRUSADES Christopher Tyerman
CRYPTOGRAPHY Fred Piper and Sean Murphy
THE CULTURAL REVOLUTION Richard Curt Kraus
DADA AND SURREALISM David Hopkins
DARWIN Jonathan Howard
THE DEAD SEA SCROLLS Timothy Lim
DEMOCRACY Bernard Crick

DERRIDA Simon Glendinning
DESCARTES Tom Sorell
DESERTS Nick Middleton
DESIGN John Heskett
DEVELOPMENTAL BIOLOGY Lewis Wolpert
THE DEVIL Darren Oldridge
DIASPORA Kevin Kenny
DICTIONARIES Lynda Mugglestone
DINOSAURS David Norman
DIPLOMACY Joseph M. Siracusa
DOCUMENTARY FILM Patricia Aufderheide
DREAMING J. Allan Hobson
DRUGS Leslie Iversen
DRUIDS Barry Cunliffe
EARLY MUSIC Thomas Forrest Kelly
THE EARTH Martin Redfern
ECONOMICS Partha Dasgupta
EDUCATION Gary Thomas
EGYPTIAN MYTH Geraldine Pinch
EIGHTEENTH-CENTURY BRITAIN Paul Langford
THE ELEMENTS Philip Ball
EMOTION Dylan Evans
EMPIRE Stephen Howe
ENGELS Terrell Carver
ENGINEERING David Blockley
ENGLISH LITERATURE Jonathan Bate
ENTREPRENEURSHIP Paul Westhead and Mike Wright
ENVIRONMENTAL ECONOMICS Stephen Smith
EPIDEMIOLOGY Rodolfo Saracci
ETHICS Simon Blackburn
THE EUROPEAN UNION John Pinder and Simon Usherwood
EVOLUTION Brian and Deborah Charlesworth
EXISTENTIALISM Thomas Flynn
FASCISM Kevin Passmore
FASHION Rebecca Arnold
FEMINISM Margaret Walters
FILM Michael Wood
FILM MUSIC Kathryn Kalinak
THE FIRST WORLD WAR Michael Howard
FOLK MUSIC Mark Slobin
FOOD John Krebs
FORENSIC PSYCHOLOGY David Canter
FORENSIC SCIENCE Jim Fraser
FOSSILS Keith Thomson
FOUCAULT Gary Gutting
FRACTALS Kenneth Falconer
FREE SPEECH Nigel Warburton
FREE WILL Thomas Pink
FRENCH LITERATURE John D. Lyons
THE FRENCH REVOLUTION William Doyle
FREUD Anthony Storr
FUNDAMENTALISM Malise Ruthven
GALAXIES John Gribbin
GALILEO Stillman Drake
GAME THEORY Ken Binmore
GANDHI Bhikhu Parekh
GENIUS Andrew Robinson
GEOGRAPHY John Matthews and David Herbert
GEOPOLITICS Klaus Dodds
GERMAN LITERATURE Nicholas Boyle
GERMAN PHILOSOPHY Andrew Bowie
GLOBAL CATASTROPHES Bill McGuire
GLOBAL ECONOMIC HISTORY Robert C. Allen
GLOBAL WARMING Mark Maslin

GLOBALIZATION Manfred Steger
THE GOTHIC Nick Groom
GOVERNANCE Mark Bevir
THE GREAT DEPRESSION AND THE NEW DEAL Eric Rauchway
HABERMAS James Gordon Finlayson
HAPPINESS Daniel M. Haybron
HEGEL Peter Singer
HEIDEGGER Michael Inwood
HERODOTUS Jennifer T. Roberts
HIEROGLYPHS Penelope Wilson
HINDUISM Kim Knott
HISTORY John H. Arnold
THE HISTORY OF ASTRONOMY Michael Hoskin
THE HISTORY OF LIFE Michael Benton
THE HISTORY OF MATHEMATICS Jacqueline Stedall
THE HISTORY OF MEDICINE William Bynum
THE HISTORY OF TIME Leofranc Holford-Strevens
HIV/AIDS Alan Whiteside
HOBBES Richard Tuck
HUMAN EVOLUTION Bernard Wood
HUMAN RIGHTS Andrew Clapham
HUMANISM Stephen Law
HUME A. J. Ayer
IDEOLOGY Michael Freeden
INDIAN PHILOSOPHY Sue Hamilton
INFORMATION Luciano Floridi
INNOVATION Mark Dodgson and David Gann
INTELLIGENCE Ian J. Deary
INTERNATIONAL MIGRATION Khalid Koser
INTERNATIONAL RELATIONS Paul Wilkinson
INTERNATIONAL SECURITY Christopher S. Browning
ISLAM Malise Ruthven
ISLAMIC HISTORY Adam Silverstein
ITALIAN LITERATURE Peter Hainsworth and David Robey
JESUS Richard Bauckham
JOURNALISM Ian Hargreaves
JUDAISM Norman Solomon
JUNG Anthony Stevens
KABBALAH Joseph Dan
KAFKA Ritchie Robertson
KANT Roger Scruton
KEYNES Robert Skidelsky
KIERKEGAARD Patrick Gardiner
THE KORAN Michael Cook
LANDSCAPES AND GEOMORPHOLOGY Andrew Goudie and Heather Viles
LANGUAGES Stephen R. Anderson
LATE ANTIQUITY Gillian Clark
LAW Raymond Wacks
THE LAWS OF THERMODYNAMICS Peter Atkins
LEADERSHIP Keith Grint
LINCOLN Allen C. Guelzo
LINGUISTICS Peter Matthews
LITERARY THEORY Jonathan Culler
LOCKE John Dunn
LOGIC Graham Priest
MACHIAVELLI Quentin Skinner
MADNESS Andrew Scull
MAGIC Owen Davies
MAGNA CARTA Nicholas Vincent
MAGNETISM Stephen Blundell
MALTHUS Donald Winch

MANAGEMENT John Hendry
MAO Delia Davin
MARINE BIOLOGY Philip V. Mladenov
THE MARQUIS DE SADE John Phillips
MARTIN LUTHER Scott H. Hendrix
MARTYRDOM Jolyon Mitchell
MARX Peter Singer
MATHEMATICS Timothy Gowers
THE MEANING OF LIFE Terry Eagleton
MEDICAL ETHICS Tony Hope
MEDICAL LAW Charles Foster
MEDIEVAL BRITAIN John Gillingham and Ralph A. Griffiths
MEMORY Jonathan K. Foster
METAPHYSICS Stephen Mumford
MICHAEL FARADAY Frank A.J.L. James
MODERN ART David Cottington
MODERN CHINA Rana Mitter
MODERN FRANCE Vanessa R. Schwartz
MODERN IRELAND Senia Pašeta
MODERN JAPAN Christopher Goto-Jones
MODERN LATIN AMERICAN LITERATURE Roberto González Echevarría
MODERN WAR Richard English
MODERNISM Christopher Butler
MOLECULES Philip Ball
THE MONGOLS Morris Rossabi
MORMONISM Richard Lyman Bushman
MUHAMMAD Jonathan A.C. Brown
MULTICULTURALISM Ali Rattansi
MUSIC Nicholas Cook
MYTH Robert A. Segal
THE NAPOLEONIC WARS Mike Rapport
NATIONALISM Steven Grosby
NELSON MANDELA Elleke Boehmer
NEOLIBERALISM Manfred Steger and Ravi Roy
NETWORKS Guido Caldarelli and Michele Catanzaro
THE NEW TESTAMENT Luke Timothy Johnson
THE NEW TESTAMENT AS LITERATURE Kyle Keefer
NEWTON Robert Iliffe
NIETZSCHE Michael Tanner
NINETEENTH-CENTURY BRITAIN Christopher Harvie and H. C. G. Matthew
THE NORMAN CONQUEST George Garnett
NORTH AMERICAN INDIANS Theda Perdue and Michael D. Green
NORTHERN IRELAND Marc Mulholland
NOTHING Frank Close
NUCLEAR POWER Maxwell Irvine
NUCLEAR WEAPONS Joseph M. Siracusa
NUMBERS Peter M. Higgins
OBJECTIVITY Stephen Gaukroger
THE OLD TESTAMENT Michael D. Coogan
THE ORCHESTRA D. Kern Holoman
ORGANIZATIONS Mary Jo Hatch
PAGANISM Owen Davies
THE PALESTINIAN-ISRAELI CONFLICT Martin Bunton
PARTICLE PHYSICS Frank Close

PAUL E. P. Sanders
PENTECOSTALISM William K. Kay
THE PERIODIC TABLE Eric R. Scerri
PHILOSOPHY Edward Craig
PHILOSOPHY OF LAW Raymond Wacks
PHILOSOPHY OF SCIENCE Samir Okasha
PHOTOGRAPHY Steve Edwards
PLAGUE Paul Slack
PLANETS David A. Rothery
PLANTS Timothy Walker
PLATO Julia Annas
POLITICAL PHILOSOPHY David Miller
POLITICS Kenneth Minogue
POSTCOLONIALISM Robert Young
POSTMODERNISM Christopher Butler
POSTSTRUCTURALISM Catherine Belsey
PREHISTORY Chris Gosden
PRESOCRATIC PHILOSOPHY Catherine Osborne
PRIVACY Raymond Wacks
PROBABILITY John Haigh
PROGRESSIVISM Walter Nugent
PROTESTANTISM Mark A. Noll
PSYCHIATRY Tom Burns
PSYCHOLOGY Gillian Butler and Freda McManus
PURITANISM Francis J. Bremer
THE QUAKERS Pink Dandelion
QUANTUM THEORY John Polkinghorne
RACISM Ali Rattansi
RADIOACTIVITY Claudio Tuniz
RASTAFARI Ennis B. Edmonds
THE REAGAN REVOLUTION Gil Troy
REALITY Jan Westerhoff
THE REFORMATION Peter Marshall
RELATIVITY Russell Stannard
RELIGION IN AMERICA Timothy Beal
THE RENAISSANCE Jerry Brotton
RENAISSANCE ART Geraldine A. Johnson
RHETORIC Richard Toye
RISK Baruch Fischhoff and John Kadvany
RIVERS Nick Middleton
ROBOTICS Alan Winfield
ROMAN BRITAIN Peter Salway
THE ROMAN EMPIRE Christopher Kelly
THE ROMAN REPUBLIC David M. Gwynn
ROMANTICISM Michael Ferber
ROUSSEAU Robert Wokler
RUSSELL A. C. Grayling
RUSSIAN HISTORY Geoffrey Hosking
RUSSIAN LITERATURE Catriona Kelly
THE RUSSIAN REVOLUTION S. A. Smith
SCHIZOPHRENIA Chris Frith and Eve Johnstone
SCHOPENHAUER Christopher Janaway
SCIENCE AND RELIGION Thomas Dixon
SCIENCE FICTION David Seed
THE SCIENTIFIC REVOLUTION Lawrence M. Principe
SCOTLAND Rab Houston
SEXUALITY Véronique Mottier
SHAKESPEARE Germaine Greer
SIKHISM Eleanor Nesbitt

THE SILK ROAD James A. Millward
SLEEP Steven W. Lockley and Russell G. Foster
SOCIAL AND CULTURAL ANTHROPOLOGY John Monaghan and Peter Just
SOCIALISM Michael Newman
SOCIOLINGUISTICS John Edwards
SOCIOLOGY Steve Bruce
SOCRATES C. C. W. Taylor
THE SOVIET UNION Stephen Lovell
THE SPANISH CIVIL WAR Helen Graham
SPANISH LITERATURE Jo Labanyi
SPINOZA Roger Scruton
SPIRITUALITY Philip Sheldrake
STARS Andrew King
STATISTICS David J. Hand
STEM CELLS Jonathan Slack
STUART BRITAIN John Morrill
SUPERCONDUCTIVITY Stephen Blundell
SYMMETRY Ian Stewart
TERRORISM Charles Townshend
THEOLOGY David F. Ford
THOMAS AQUINAS Fergus Kerr
THOUGHT Tim Bayne
TIBETAN BUDDHISM Matthew T. Kapstein
TOCQUEVILLE Harvey C. Mansfield
TRAGEDY Adrian Poole
THE TROJAN WAR Eric H. Cline
TRUST Katherine Hawley
THE TUDORS John Guy
TWENTIETH-CENTURY BRITAIN Kenneth O. Morgan
THE UNITED NATIONS Jussi M. Hanhimäki
THE U.S. CONGRESS Donald A. Ritchie
THE U.S. SUPREME COURT Linda Greenhouse
UTOPIANISM Lyman Tower Sargent
THE VIKINGS Julian Richards
VIRUSES Dorothy H. Crawford
WITCHCRAFT Malcolm Gaskill
WITTGENSTEIN A. C. Grayling
WORK Stephen Fineman
WORLD MUSIC Philip Bohlman
THE WORLD TRADE ORGANIZATION Amrita Narlikar
WRITING AND SCRIPT Andrew Robinson

Available soon:

BLACK HOLES Katherine Blundell
HUMOUR Noel Carroll
AMERICAN LEGAL HISTORY G. Edward White
REVOLUTIONS Jack A. Goldstone
FAMILY LAW Jonathan Herring

For more information visit our web site

www.oup.co.uk/general/vsi/

Amanda H. Podany

THE ANCIENT NEAR EAST

A Very Short Introduction

OXFORD
UNIVERSITY PRESS

Oxford University Press is a department of the University of Oxford. It furthers the University's objective of excellence in research, scholarship, and education by publishing worldwide.

Oxford New York
Auckland Cape Town Dar es Salaam Hong Kong Karachi Kuala Lumpur Madrid Melbourne Mexico City Nairobi New Delhi Shanghai Taipei Toronto

With offices in
Argentina Austria Brazil Chile Czech Republic France Greece Guatemala Hungary Italy Japan Poland Portugal Singapore South Korea Switzerland Thailand Turkey Ukraine Vietnam

Oxford is a registered trademark of Oxford University Press in the UK and certain other countries.

Published in the United States of America by
Oxford University Press
198 Madison Avenue, New York, NY 10016

Library of Congress Cataloging-in-Publication Data
Podany, Amanda H.
The Ancient Near East : a very short introduction / Amanda Podany.
pages cm.—Very short introductions
Includes bibliographical references and index.
ISBN 978-0-19-537799-6 (alk. paper)
1. Middle East—History—To 622. I. Title.
DS62.23.P625 2013
939.4—dc23 2013009337

Printed in Great Britain
by Ashford Colour Press Ltd., Gosport, Hants.
on acid-free paper

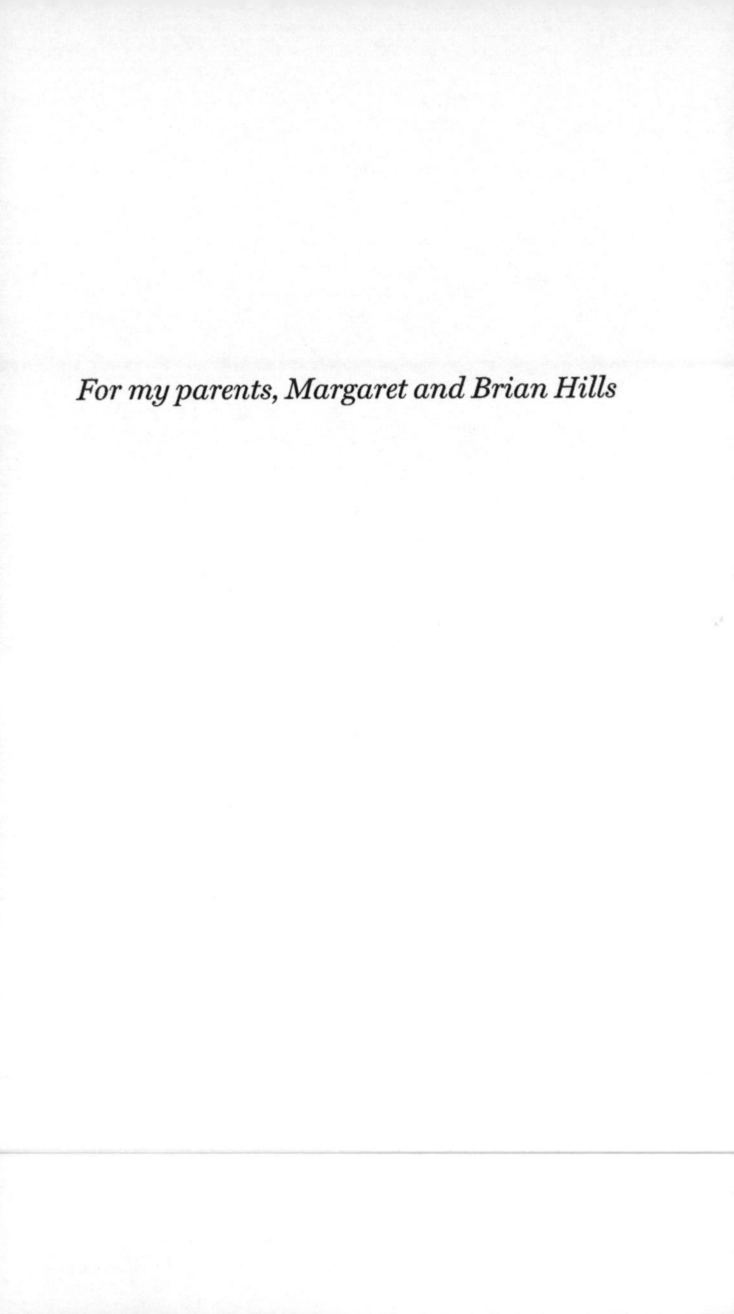

For my parents, Margaret and Brian Hills

Contents

List of illustrations xv

Note on translations xvii

Acknowledgments xix

1 Archaeology and environment 1

2 The beginning of cities, 3600–2900 BCE 16

3 The Early Dynastic period, 2900–2334 BCE 27

4 The Akkadian Empire, 2334–2193 BCE 40

5 The Third Dynasty of Ur, 2193–2004 BCE 51

6 The Old Assyrian colonies, 1950–1740 BCE 63

7 The Old Babylonian period, 2004–1595 BCE 74

8 The Late Bronze Age, 1595–1155 BCE 87

9 The Neo-Assyrian Empire, 972–612 BCE 100

10 The Neo-Babylonian Empire, 612–539 BCE 112

Chronology 125

References 127

Further reading 131

Index 137

List of illustrations

1. Map of the ancient Near East, 3500–539 BCE. 12
2. Map of major Mesopotamian cities, 3500–539 BCE. 14
3. Proto-cuneiform tablet from Uruk. Hans Nissen, "The Archaic Texts from Uruk," *World Archaeology* 17 (1986). From the Warka Collection of the University of Heidelberg with permission from Hans Nissen. 18
4. Relief sculpture of King Enannatum of Lagash. 30
   © Trustees of the British Museum
5. Detail of relief sculpture from the victory stela of King Naram-Sin of Akkad. Gianni Dagli Orti/Art Archive at Art Resource, NY. With permission from Art Resource. 49
6. Copper alloy figure of King Ur-Namma of Ur. 54
   © Trustees of the British Museum.
7. Cuneiform letter from Assyrian merchant Assur-idi. Erich Lessing/Art Resource, NY. With permission from Art Resource. 71
8. Diorite relief sculpture from the top of the stela containing Hammurabi's laws. ©RMN-Grand Palais/Art Resource, NY. With permission from Art Resource. 78
9. Syrian cylinder seal from the Late Bronze Age. 95
   © Trustees of the British Museum.
10. Relief sculpture from a palace wall of Assurnasirpal II. 104
    © Trustees of the British Museum.
11. Clay cylinder recording Nabonidus's reconstruction of three temples. 117
    © Trustees of the British Museum.

Note on translations

All quoted texts and proper names were originally written in the cuneiform script and in ancient languages (Akkadian, Sumerian, and Hittite). In scholarly translations of the ancient texts, certain sounds are normally represented by diacritics (e.g., ṣ, š, ṭ, ḫ). These symbols have been replaced in this book with their closest equivalents in the Roman alphabet.

The spellings used for proper names also vary among scholars; I have attempted to use the most common form for each name.

Because cuneiform tablets are often broken or damaged, texts are rarely complete. It is conventional, in publications of cuneiform texts, to enclose reconstructed sections in brackets ([. . .]). I have omitted these brackets in translations only where the reconstructions are obvious and not controversial.

Another translation convention, followed here, is to add words that were not used in the ancient languages in order to clarify the meaning of a text. These words are placed in parentheses within the quotation.

Acknowledgments

When Nancy Toff asked me if I would be interested in writing this book, I knew it would be a fascinating challenge, and I was delighted to say yes. I'm indebted to her for all her help and advice as my editor and friend. Thanks also to the others at OUP who have also contributed to the process of producing this book, including Joellyn Ausanka, Gwen Gethner, Max Richman, and Mary Sutherland; to Steven Garfinkle and Gary Beckman for advice on specific chapters; to several anonymous reviewers for their excellent suggestions; and to Hans Nissen for permission to use his autograph copy of the proto-cuneiform text. As always, I appreciate the support of my wonderful colleagues in the History Department and the College of Letters, Arts, and Social Sciences at Cal Poly Pomona, including Dean Sharon Hilles. I am dedicating this book with much love to my parents, Margaret and Brian Hills, who encouraged my interest in the ancient world from my childhood. And to my family, Jerry, Emily, and Nick: you are the best.

Chapter 1
Archaeology and environment

Civilization in the ancient Near East was both long lasting and successful. The three thousand years from 3600 to 539 BCE encompass an era of remarkable innovation and achievement. The region is known as the "cradle of civilization" for good reason. Here, men and women first tried to live peacefully together in densely urban cities and found ways, through law and custom, to thrive and prosper. The popular image of history as a story of progress from primitive barbarism to modern sophistication is completely belied by the study of the ancient Near East. For example, women in early times had many rights and freedoms: they could own property, run businesses, and represent themselves in court. Diplomats traveled between the capital cities of major powers ensuring peace and friendship between the kings. Scribes and scholars studied the stars and could predict eclipses and the movements of the planets. Some of these achievements were lost in subsequent centuries, only to be reborn in more modern times.

Perhaps the most obvious legacy from the ancient Near East is seen in some of our units of measurement. The Mesopotamians invented a mathematical system based on the number sixty, and all the sixty-based units in our modern world (including seconds, minutes, and degrees) have come down to us, in some way or another, from Mesopotamia. Other legacies arrived in a more circuitous fashion. Law, for example, once invented in

Mesopotamia around 2100 BCE, was never forgotten, even though the actual laws of the Mesopotamians bear little resemblance to those in use today. Echoes of the ancient Near Eastern civilizations can be seen all around us.

The ancient Near East is fascinating and important not only for the enormous impact it had on subsequent civilizations but also for the way in which its history was lost for centuries, reemerging as the result of archaeological excavations and the decipherment of ancient scripts. The history is far from complete, and it changes subtly every year as new objects and texts are found and old ones are reinterpreted. What can be included in any history of the ancient Near East is determined almost entirely by what has been found in the ground. Very little memory of the civilization survived over the centuries after its collapse beyond a few references in the Bible and in the works of a handful of Greek and Roman authors. Until archaeological excavations began and the ancient cuneiform script was deciphered in the nineteenth century, almost no one guessed how significant the ancient Near East was to the history of the world.

Archaeological evidence

In some ways we are tremendously lucky with regard to the accidents of history that left us archaeological evidence of ancient Near Eastern peoples. For many cultures, much less is known, much less survives.

One great advantage for the preservation of the civilization was that in parts of the Near East, particularly in southern Mesopotamia where many of the earliest cities were built, little stone or wood was available. The hot, dry climate of southern Mesopotamia did not allow for the growth of the types of tall, straight pine and cedar trees that were best for construction. Any such logs had to be imported. That was bad for the Mesopotamians but good for us, because they used wood only where it was absolutely needed (in roofing and doors, for example) and found ways of being highly creative in their use of mud and clay. They built with it, made pots out of it, grew their crops in it, and wrote on it. Unlike wood, clay does not decompose. It also, fortunately, is not particularly recyclable. Whereas wooden logs or stone blocks could be reused in one building after another, a crumbling mud brick wall tended to get knocked over (leaving a foot or two of wall standing), the bricks leveled within what had been the room in order to create a new floor, and the floor then stamped down. New mud bricks were brought in to construct the walls of the new structure. And so, in much of the Near East, the ground level in villages and cities gradually rose as one generation after another built their homes on top of the leveled remains of older buildings. Rarely did anyone ever destroy those ancient levels; they were preserved simply by being ignored.

Among the debris on the floors of forgotten buildings, encased in mud beneath later levels (not just of homes but of palaces, temples, government offices, workshops, and so on), was the trash that no one had cared enough about to save or remove. Broken pots were useless. They were strewn around many floors, along with food waste, old baskets and mats, and documents that were out of date, no longer relevant, and often broken. These included letters about issues long since resolved, contracts for property purchased by parents or grandparents, school exercises, lists of people who had worked together on forgotten projects, loans already paid off . . . we have similar records in our own houses today. But because the people of the ancient Near East wrote on clay, many of the documents survived (especially if the house burned down, fortuitously baking the clay). Much of the debris and detritus of daily life, including such documents, were abandoned and buried as one level of construction was built on top of the one before it, over and over again.

Hundreds of huge mounds (called tells) were thereby created over centuries or millennia, in which the lowest levels entomb materials from the earliest settlements and the top levels hold debris from the most recent eras of occupation. Sometimes the site was never abandoned, and a city still thrives on top of and around the ancient tell. The modern cities of Aleppo, Damascus, and Erbil, for example, each has at its heart a tell marking the original location of the city that has flourished there for thousands of years.

Inside each undisturbed mound are all the stratigraphic remains of walls and floors and streets of past communities, every object and document in place just where it was abandoned (unless disturbed by animals or by pits dug by later inhabitants). It might not be as perfect a time capsule as a city covered in volcanic ash, like Pompeii, but every tell is a storehouse of information, locked up hundreds or thousands of years ago.

Excavators, when they take to working on such untouched tells, can ideally extract a great deal of knowledge about the ancient community while doing the minimum amount of damage. Study of the stratigraphy—the occupation layers below the present ground level of the site—allows archaeologists to place objects and buildings in time as well as in space. The information comes out very slowly—modern excavations are often glacial in pace as the archaeologists record every wall, every object, every ash layer—but little is missed. Using remote sensing, photography, and careful analysis of the organic remains, artifacts, and buildings as they are uncovered, archaeologists and historians are able to rediscover vast amounts of information. This ranges from the contents of pots, which inform us about what people ate, to the ways that documents were organized in archives, to the uses to which rooms were put, to the layout of a whole neighborhood (which is occasionally possible without even uncovering it). Historians and epigraphists can read and analyze the documents found, sometimes identifying the names of the people who worked and lived in the buildings, learning about their concerns, their religious beliefs, their relationships with their neighbors, their marriages and children, and their work for the state or the temple. Whole communities spring back to life through the meticulous study of such details.

Regrettably, though, we do not have this luxury for many of the ancient Near Eastern cities. Most are far from untouched. Some of the largest and most important tells have been ravaged for more than two centuries, first by early archaeologists who knew no better, and later by treasure hunters and looters. Some of the digging crews blew through the sites like tornados, plowing through all the rooms and streets, palaces and temples, destroying walls and floors, throwing aside anything but the objects that were deemed museum-worthy or that could be sold for a profit, leaving a wasteland where once there had been a fragile time capsule. Looters still get to many sites before the archaeologists have a chance to excavate carefully, especially in Iraq and Syria as a result of the wars there. Some sites are as cratered as the surface of the moon by the pits of the looters.

The tragedy of all this is that nothing that has been destroyed in the course of digging or looting can ever be recovered. Much of the knowledge that could have been obtained from these ancient towns and cities is lost forever.

Understanding the ancient Near East will always be vital to an overview of human history. No matter how many millennia stretch out ahead for civilization, its beginning (the first writing, the first cities, the first laws, and so on) will always lie in the Near East. What has been lost is lost not just to us but to all humankind in the future. The story of the origins of civilization will forever be less complete than it could have been had those sites been excavated methodically and not looted.

Between the extremes of careful excavation and wanton looting are sites where, for various reasons, some vital information (though not all) has been lost to modern scholars. Some were excavated well, given the technology of the times, but the excavations took place before modern techniques developed. Some ancient cities were dug too fast, or the excavator hired hundreds of workmen, not allowing for adequate records to be kept of what was found. In some cases, mud brick walls were not recognized as such and were destroyed. Some sites have been sacrificed to the need for water and hydroelectric power as dams have been built on the venerable rivers, and the reservoirs they created have drowned ancient cities. In such cases rescue excavations have often been mounted to preserve as much as can be found over the course of a limited number of excavation seasons, but the majority of the material from such a tell ends up underwater. Not only has a great deal of information been lost to looters and early archaeology, but what is available to us now is only a fraction compared with what is still buried, awaiting discovery by future archaeologists (who will presumably have even better ways of preserving and extracting information from the physical evidence that they find).

A history of the ancient Near East is therefore strangely dependent on what happens to have been recovered from the ground and on when and by whom it was recovered. Modern scholars follow along in the wake of the early enthusiasts (and thieves), piecing together a history from what they left behind, learning as much as possible from the objects, the tablets, and the excavation records, such as they are. These conclusions they combine with what has been deduced from modern excavations in order to come up with a portrait of the ancient Near East. The political history that results is sketchy, even for the kings and states about which we know the most. Future historians will certainly be better informed about the ancient Near East than we are now.

Geography, climate, and natural resources

The ancient Near East is defined here as comprising the "cuneiform lands," that is, the regions of the ancient world where the cuneiform script (made up of short wedge-topped lines combined into symbols), written mostly on clay tablets, was used as the most common medium for written communication. These lands were Mesopotamia (modern Iraq, with its variously named regions: Sumer, Akkad, Babylonia, and Assyria), Syria, Elam (part of what was later known as Persia), and Anatolia (modern Turkey). Although cuneiform was occasionally employed in both Canaan and Egypt, they had other writing systems that were more widely used, and they are discussed in this book only in the context of their trade and diplomatic relationships with the cuneiform lands.

The use of cuneiform is not an arbitrary distinction between ancient civilizations; the cuneiform lands had much more in common than simply the use of the same script. From the very beginning of urban civilization in the fourth millennium BCE, the lands of Mesopotamia, Syria, and Elam were in close contact with one another, because the first southern Mesopotamian cities established colonies in the lands to their north and east. In later millennia the peoples of these three regions were sometime allies, sometime enemies, and constant trading partners. Mesopotamia and Syria were occasionally united into a single empire, though Elam tended to remain outside such larger states.

Anatolia was not a stranger to the cuneiform lands, even in the third millennium BCE. In later centuries, Anatolian legends maintained that the great Akkadian King Sargon had ventured onto the Anatolian plateau during his campaigns in the twenty-fourth century BCE. The local people had a sophisticated urban culture, and they traded with the lands around them, including Mesopotamia and Syria. In the early second millennium BCE Anatolia joined the cuneiform world. The script was initially introduced by traders from Assyria, and a few centuries later it was adopted wholeheartedly by the local Hittite kings and their administrators. The Hittites assumed many of the cultural conventions of their southern neighbors, such as communicating through letters, establishing treaties with allies, maintaining palace and temple archives of administrative and religious documents, and ruling with the assistance of bureaucrats, governors, and vassal kings.

Although the cuneiform lands shared many aspects of their culture, geographically they were distinct. The climate and physical landscape have not changed all that much since ancient times so one can get a sense of the ancient places from exploring the regions as they are now.

Southern Mesopotamia would be an uninhabitable desert were it not for the two rivers that weave across its flat expanse. The fast-flowing Tigris and somewhat slower Euphrates laid down the silt through which they flow. Lacking rocky riverbeds, the rivers have always been fickle, apt to change course completely after a flood. They now flow far from the ancient cities that used to depend on them. The Mesopotamian people tamed and domesticated the rivers, particularly the Euphrates, bringing its great force under control and using its waters for many of their needs—they irrigated their fields from it, sailed boats full of cargo and people on it, washed in it, drank it (though they preferred beer), fished in it, and used it as a moat for their cities.

Although some catastrophic floods probably took place in the times of the very earliest settlements, perhaps destroying communities and burying them under feet of mud, and although vague memories of those floods influenced myths and legends, the Mesopotamians seem not to have suffered too much from flooding of the rivers after cities were established. Later letters, inscriptions, and prayers, in which one might expect to see frequent references to flooding if it had been a major concern, mostly describe the rivers as a blessing. After all, rain was scarce, but river water seemed to be an inexhaustible and reliable gift.

Regions to the north, east, and west of southern Mesopotamia enjoyed more rainfall and depended less on rivers. In Syria to the northwest and Assyria to the northeast the rivers mostly flowed through rock and were less likely to change course. Farms did not need to be right next to the rivers. Watered by the rain, they could extend across the plains and into the hills, sometimes replacing the natural woodlands of pistachio and oak trees. In Anatolia to the north and parts of Elam to the east, mountains and plateaus made for land that was difficult to traverse and, in places, to farm. Peoples living in the mountains were notoriously hard to rein in to any large kingdom or empire. When powers in the plains began to weaken, it was often forces from the mountains that swept in to deliver the final blow to their dynasties.

Many of the cuneiform lands were landlocked. Although the Mesopotamian cities in the far south had access to the Persian Gulf, and the port cities of western Syria faced the Mediterranean, most Mesopotamian and Syrian city-states and later kingdoms had no coastline. Anatolia was cut off from the Mediterranean Sea by the Taurus Mountains; only the coastal plain known as Kizzuwatna (later Cilicia) to the southeast of Anatolia had useful harbors. So most of the communication among the cuneiform lands took place overland or by river.

Natural resources were unevenly distributed as well. Southern Mesopotamia had the most dependable crops, and it had salt, along with bitumen used for waterproofing boats, but it had stone only in a few places and no metal ores. It was not poor, however. Vast herds of sheep, which are mentioned in texts from all eras, produced abundant wool that was spun and woven into fine textiles. These were central to the Mesopotamian economy and were traded widely.

Parts of Syria were forested; one area was known as the "cedar mountain" in Mesopotamian mythology. Anatolians had silver and copper ore in their mountains, along with obsidian. Elam was on the trade route that brought copper from central Iran, lapis lazuli (a semiprecious blue stone) and tin from Afghanistan, carnelian and shells from the Indus Valley, and perhaps gold from eastern Iran or Pakistan. Eventually, trade in these various commodities brought the lands into close contact with one another.

Scope and approach of this book

Of the hundreds of thousands of cuneiform documents that have been excavated from ancient Near Eastern sites, this book focuses on just thirty-three texts that represent their times, places, and cultures particularly well. They include administrative lists, royal inscriptions, hymns, laws, treaties, letters, contracts, prayers, literary works, and names assigned to years. Each quoted document provides a window into the ancient Near Eastern world, giving details of the era in which it was written along with insights into such matters as the relationship between the gods and the people (particularly the kings), trade, religion, diplomacy, law, agriculture, warfare, kingship, society, and agriculture. In many cases, the site where the document was uncovered is also discussed, the archaeological context providing a richer understanding of the time and place in which it was written.

The widely used Middle Chronology—which gives the dates of Hammurabi's reign as 1792 to 1750 BCE—is followed in this book. Dates after ca. 1400 BCE are fairly reliable and uncontroversial (the more recent, the less controversial). For dates before 1500 BCE, however, a debate revolves around the Middle Chronology. Some scholars propose lower dates (from eight years to as much as a century later). But until a consensus is reached, it seems best to use the dates that are familiar, if probably wrong.

The book begins around 3600 BCE with the first Mesopotamian cities (which coincide with the invention of writing) and ends with the conquest of the Near East by the Persian king Cyrus the Great in 539 BCE. Although cuneiform did not go out of use at this time, the Persian conquest marked the end of an era. By 539 BCE, Elam had been subsumed into the Persian heartland and had ceased to exist as an independent power. No longer were Mesopotamia, Syria, and Anatolia ruled by local kings; they became provinces of the larger Persian Empire. The main language spoken across the Near East was now Aramaic, which was written not in cuneiform on clay tablets but in an alphabetic script on papyrus or parchment. Much of the culture that had accompanied the use of cuneiform—including religious beliefs, governmental structures, and economic realities—began to change, and within a few centuries was completely transformed.

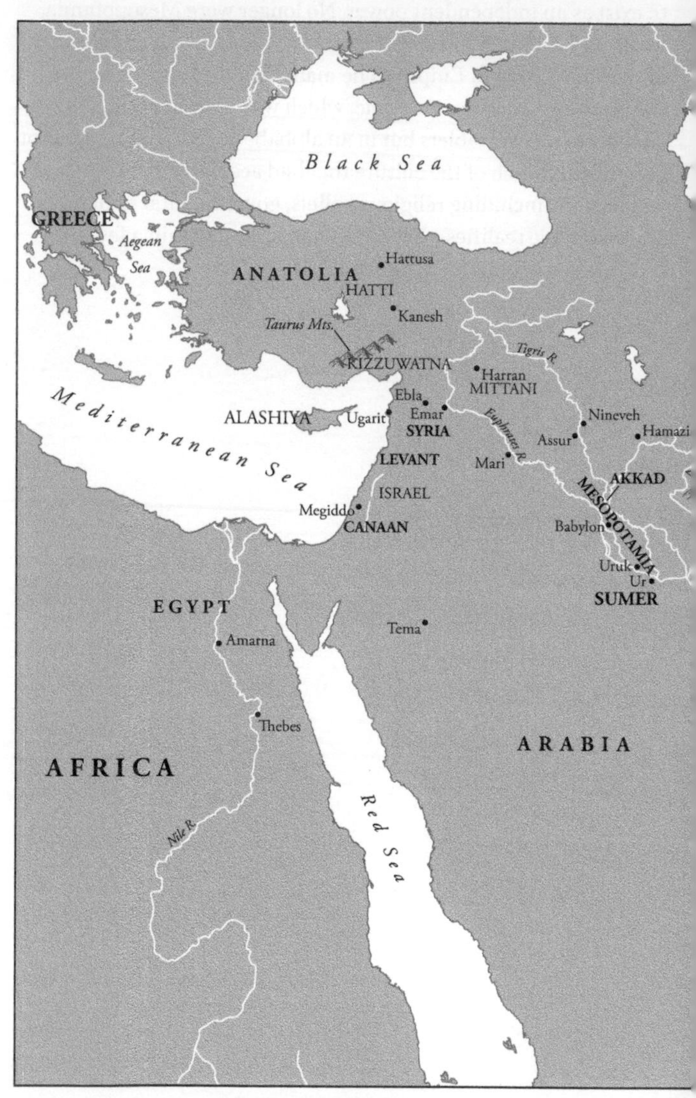

1. Map of the ancient Near East and surrounding regions, 3500–539 BCE.

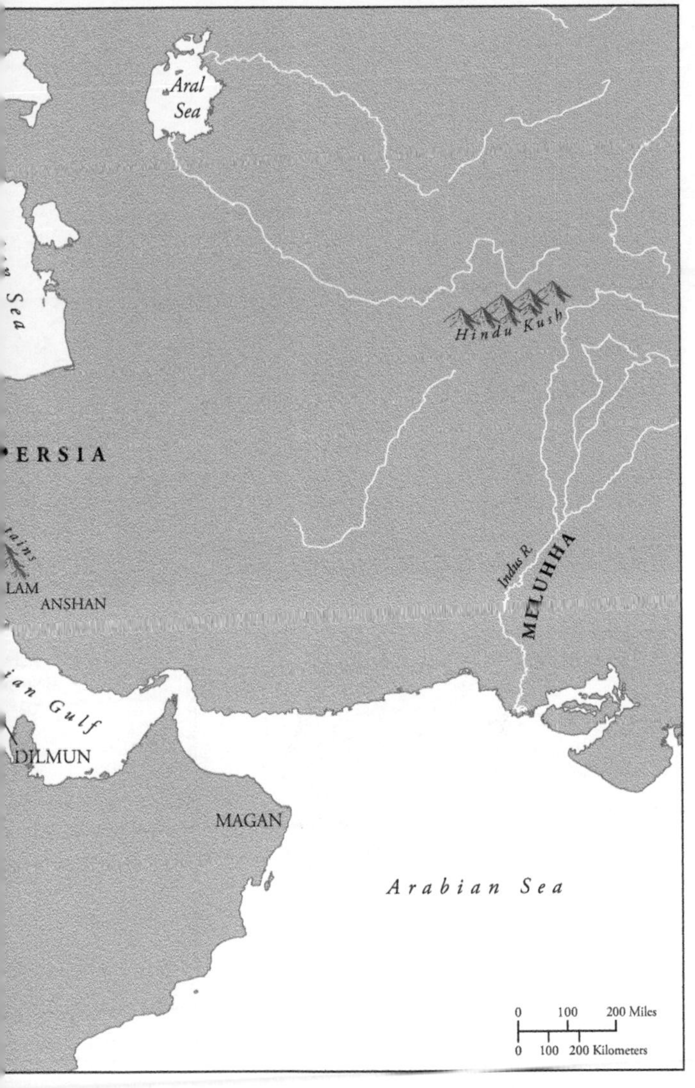

Aral Sea
Hindu Kush
ERSIA
LAM
ANSHAN
Indus R.
MELUHHA
Gulf
DILMUN
MAGAN
Arabian Sea
0 100 200 Miles
0 100 200 Kilometers

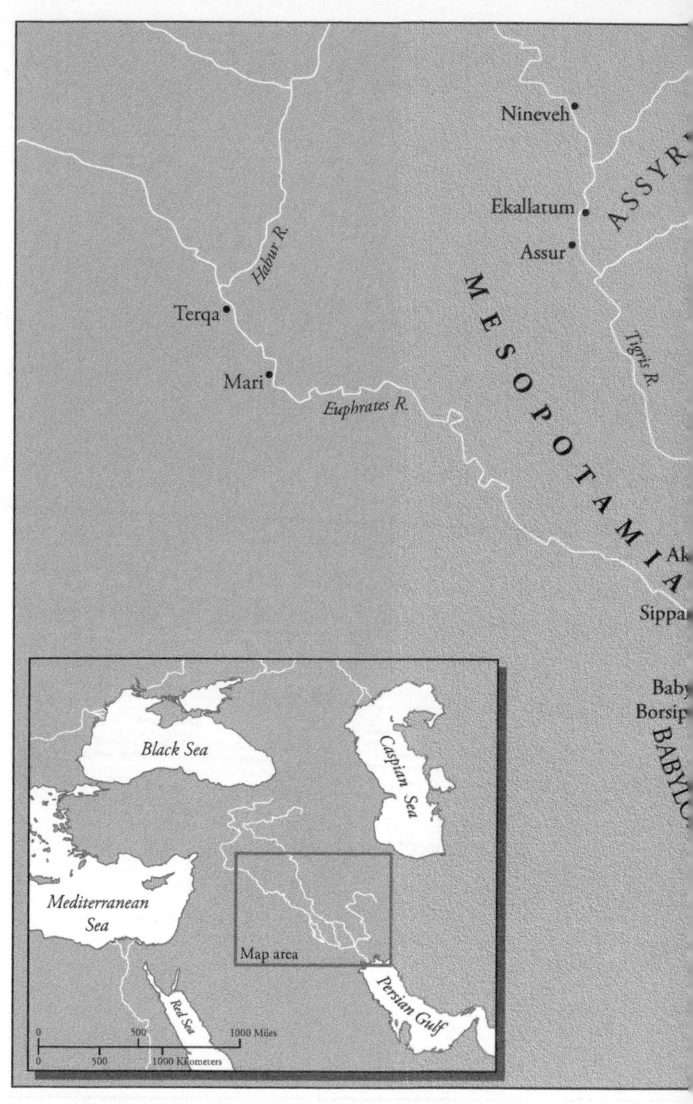

2. Map of major Mesopotamian cities, 3500–539 BCE.

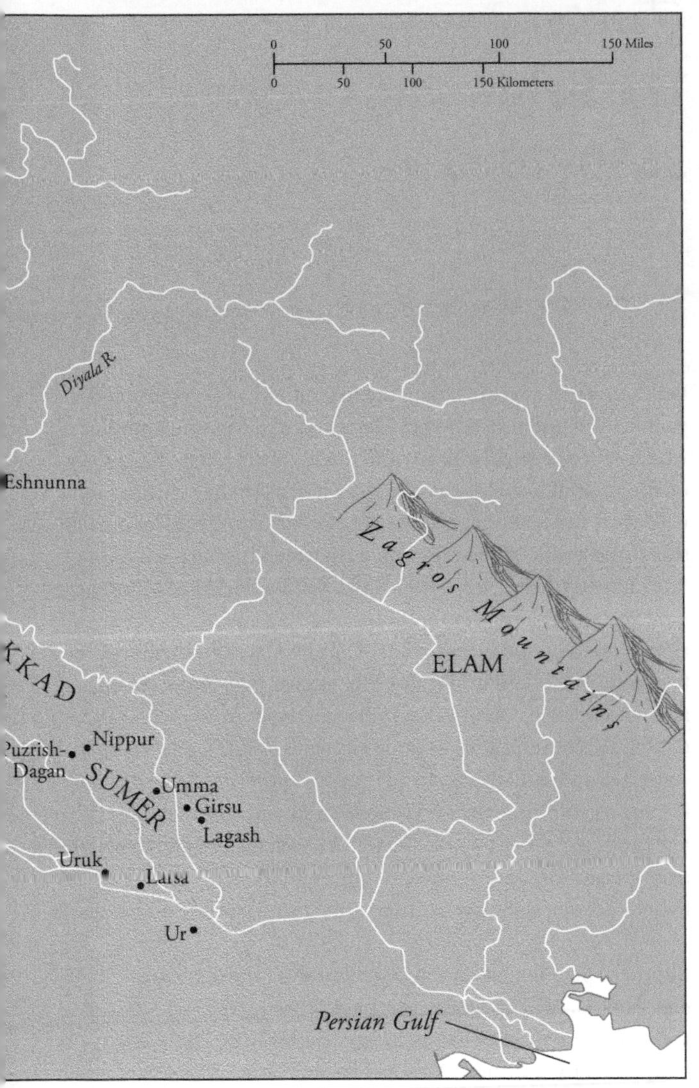
0
50
100
150 Miles
0
50
100
150 Kilometers
Diyala R.
Eshnunna
Zagros Mountains
ELAM
KKAD
Nippur
Puzrish-
Dagan
SUMER
Umma
Girsu
Lagash
Uruk
Larsa
Ur
Persian Gulf

Chapter 2
The beginning of cities, 3600–2900 BCE

For thousands of years before the first cities were constructed, people lived and prospered in Mesopotamia. Farming families who dwelled in small villages and towns in the north depended on the rainfall to water their crops, whereas in the south farmers used river water. Across the region, herders cared for flocks of sheep and goats. Men and women perfected the arts of making fine pottery, textiles, and stone tools. With sun-dried bricks they built rectangular houses for themselves and shrines for their gods, always on the same sacred spots. They buried their dead with goods that would be of use in the afterlife, such as pots and weapons, and with luxuries, such as sea shells and gold, from distant places. Gradually, communities became larger, as did the temples at their centers. Successful agricultural practices permitted more people to live together. The social and economic advantages of living with a few thousand other people—as well as perhaps the benefits of living near the gods in their temples—outweighed the disadvantages of living in close proximity to others: the noises, smells, and diseases.

But these people had no way to record their thoughts or experiences. All knowledge was passed orally from one person and one generation to the next, so we know little about them. Only when the southern Mesopotamian communities expanded to become cities did someone come up with a system to capture all the facts needed to administer the communities, facts that no one could conceivably commit to memory. And with this system—writing—scribes gradually increased the types of information that they recorded, leaving a record for the future.

The city of Uruk

Uruk in 3100 BCE was vastly bigger than any community that had existed before, not just in Mesopotamia but, as far as we know, anywhere. It was enclosed by a city wall ten kilometers around, and may have had a population of as many as twenty-five thousand. The goddess Inanna served as patron deity and queen of the city. Her house, or temple (the word for both was the same in ancient Mesopotamia), was Uruk's most important structure. As far as the residents were concerned, the gods themselves had constructed the earliest version of her temple on this sacred spot; humans were a later addition to the city, put there to serve her. Inanna, goddess of both war and love, was worshiped in other cities as well, but Uruk was her home. It remained so until the end of Mesopotamian civilization, thousands of years later, until Inanna had no more worshipers.

A fragmentary tablet inscribed bearing a sequence of word signs was found in the remains of Inanna's temple in Uruk, one of a number that were found there. It was written around 3100 BCE, when writing was still a relatively new concept, and it provides an early glimpse into the economy and religion of the Mesopotamian people. It reads "2. Temple. Sheep. God. Inanna." Or perhaps "2. Sheep. God. Inanna. Temple." A scribe had impressed the signs on the clay tablet using a stylus, not for his own edification but on behalf of the institution where he worked. Like most documents written in this early time, its meaning is hard to fathom. It is written in a script known as proto-cuneiform, a script that did not represent sounds or even language at all; signs served as memory aids. At the top left of the tablet are two half-ovals, each representing the number one. At the top right is a sign that stood for a temple or house. In the center, the circle with a cross through

3. This proto-cuneiform tablet from Uruk includes signs for sheep and the goddess Inanna, but its meaning is unclear.

it signified "sheep." Below that is a star. This either indicated the god of the heavens, An, or the idea of a "god" or "goddess." And below that is a complicated sign for the goddess Inanna. One possible translation is "Two sheep (delivered to) the temple of the goddess Inanna."

The temple to which the two sheep were to be delivered was presumably the one where the tablet was found (in a pile of rubbish brought in to level a floor, not in an archive). This structure was known later as the Eanna, literally the "house of heaven." The scale and complexity of the temple precinct would be impressive even for a modern structure; one can only wonder how extraordinary it must have seemed to a visitor in the fourth millennium BCE. At least seven large buildings (several of them separate temples) and a square courtyard sixty meters on each side dominated the walled complex. Most of the buildings were more than fifty meters (about 165 feet) long, each of them finely constructed of brick and limestone. One building had columns (the earliest known columns anywhere), but the builders seem to have been unsure of this new technology, not certain that it could be trusted to hold up the roof; the columns were two meters wide, with little space between them. Some of the walls and columns dazzled the eye, covered with bright mosaics of red, white, and black circles set in patterns: herringbones, diamonds, and stripes. (The colored circles of which they were constructed were the flat ends of cones pressed into plaster; some of them made of stone, others of clay.)

The investment of time and manpower devoted to the construction of this complex would have resembled the work on a medieval cathedral. As early as 3600 BCE work had begun on the so-called Limestone Temple in the Eanna precinct. Quarrymen and masons removed limestone from a rocky outcrop around fifty kilometers (31 mi) to the southwest. Other men transported the stone to Uruk. Still others formed hundreds of thousands of mud bricks and clay cones, and set them out to harden in the sun. Others brought timber from far to the north for the roofs. Someone supervised all the workmen who set the bricks and stones and mosaic cones in place. The men would have been fed and provided for during the construction. The builders were all probably residents of Uruk, united in their desire to create a magnificent home for their beloved divine queen.

Many economic documents from Uruk record rations, presumably for such workmen and for countless others (men and women) employed by the temple after its construction. They received bread and beer, larger quantities for supervisors and smaller amounts for hired men (and smaller amounts still for women). Already society was stratified, with wealth and power unequally allocated. The rations were distributed in coarse, mold-made, triangular bowls, referred to as beveled-rim bowls, which are found in vast quantities at Uruk and at other sites from the same era. The sign for "food" (also for "bread") in proto-cuneiform is the shape of a beveled-rim bowl.

But who brought the workers together to undertake the construction? Who ruled over them? Who organized their assignments and made sure they all got compensated? Who had all the beveled-rim bowls made and filled with bread and beer? Did the people of Uruk have a king? Scholars think that they probably did not, at least not this early. There were no recognizable palaces, for one thing. And there seems to have been no word for "king" yet. An indication of this is seen in some of the earliest documents, which were simple lists of words in categories, perhaps to help scribes learn to write. One of these listed professions. The most important roles seem to have been listed first, but there was no king among them. The later terms for a king were "lugal" or "en"—these terms don't appear on the list. It could be that priests were in charge. After all, they had the closest ties to the gods.

The goddess Inanna

As for Inanna herself, she was housed safely in one of the temple structures. A lovely white marble sculpture of a woman's face was found in the early levels of the Eanna; this life-sized representation might even have been from Inanna's cult statue. Her hair, eyebrows, and eyes would have been inlaid with other materials such as gold, bitumen, and lapis lazuli. Like all the gods and goddesses, each of whom had a city to call home, Inanna had a physical form—her cult statue—as well as a cosmic presence. The rest of her statue might have been made of gold or of gold-plated wood, and it would have been dressed in elaborate jewelry and robes. She was a fickle, sometimes imperious, goddess, according to the stories about her written down by later scribes. Her priests would have wanted to keep her happy.

One way to keep the gods and goddesses happy was to provide them with regular meals. The two sheep listed in the economic document might have been for this purpose. Just like humans, the gods enjoyed feasting, so meat, beer, bread, vegetables, and fruits were laid out for them several times a day.

Proto-cuneiform writing and cylinder seals

The fragmentary economic tablet recorded that these two sheep had some relationship to Inanna's temple. But it is not a particularly useful document, to modern eyes. Even if it were complete, we know from other examples that there would have been no date. When were the sheep delivered? Were they, indeed, delivered? The text, like others of this era, has no verb. Could the sheep instead have been taken away from the temple? Who delivered the sheep? Was this a required tax or a voluntary donation? Or did the sheep belong to the temple? Who received the sheep? For bookkeeping purposes, the tablet seems inadequate. An archive of such documents would be untethered from the time, purpose, or individuals involved in their creation. This is true unless, perhaps, such documents were placed in specific baskets or boxes that provided the additional information (e.g., all the tablets in one box might have recorded sheep delivered on a particular day or from a particular herd).

Other proto-cuneiform documents are often even harder to read than this one. Most seem to have listed nothing but numbers and nouns. The people of Uruk started out with at least thirteen different numerical systems; they counted differently depending on what they were counting, and the signs indicated different numbers for different commodities. And about 30 percent of the signs they first created to represent nouns had no later equivalents, so scholars do not know how to read them.

More than five thousand proto-cuneiform tablets have been uncovered, the majority of them, like this one, from Uruk. Most of them—85 percent, in fact—are economic. The other 15 percent are lexical lists in which words were grouped in broad categories. In addition to the list of professions there were lists of places, objects made of wood, body parts, and many others. But the scribes of Uruk did not write anything creative or reflective. They did not even write letters to one another. Those came later. Their writing system almost certainly had developed as a memory aid for officials charged with running a large organization. They needed to keep track of quantities of sheep, goats, textiles, foodstuffs, cattle, and the like. The temples seem to have owned or controlled vast amounts of land and animals. A few earlier attempts at creating a system to help with the impossible task of remembering details about these properties had proved less satisfactory. Officials had tried making small tokens (one to represent each item) and putting them in a bowl, or sealing them in a clay ball, or impressing them on a piece of clay. They had varied the shapes of the tokens, one shape for a sheep, one for a pitcher of beer, one for a sheaf of wheat, and so on. But drawing a sign on clay for each word and adding symbols for numerals seems to have worked much better.

In fact, this economic text is far from being one of the earliest. The signs on it were impressed with a stylus with a straight edge (other than for the curve of the "sheep" sign). In the earliest documents, a century or so before this one, the signs looked more like pictures and were incised into the clay with a sharp, pointed stylus.

Over time, economic documents became more complex and more informative. Scribes began to identify the persons involved in transactions, either by profession (the priest of Inanna, for example) or even by name. Names could be written somewhat phonetically, using pictures of objects that sounded like the name. The scribes added totals of goods distributed to different persons and included the sum at the end. Some of the tablets listed place names (they can be recognized because the spelling did not change much over time), often of Uruk itself, but also of surrounding cities such as Ur and distant cities like Kish, with which the people of Uruk were in contact. A few documents even mentioned the far-off land of Dilmun, way to the south across the Persian Gulf in what is now Bahrain.

In the later Uruk documents there was still no logical order for the signs—they were not written in the sequence in which the words were spoken. The scribes do not seem to have thought of this script that they had invented as a representation of language.

One other form of visual communication arose in Uruk at around the same time: the cylinder seal. It became the artifact that was perhaps most characteristic of Mesopotamia, useful in many ways and also one of the most visually arresting objects produced by craftsmen in any era. A cylinder seal was a stone cylindrical bead carved in relief with a scene, so that when rolled on a piece of clay it produced an endless tiny frieze of figures or patterns. Men and women of importance owned private cylinder seals and rolled them on clay documents to attest to their involvement in a transaction. Even more often they would use the cylinders to seal objects. A shipment needed to be secured against theft? Plaster the top with a piece of clay and seal it. The recipient of the container would know whether the shipment had been broken into and who had sent it. Cylinder seals were used for thousands of years in Mesopotamia and Syria.

The Uruk period

Uruk is the largest city that has been excavated from the late fourth millennium BCE in Mesopotamia, but a number of other settlements had the same type of monumental architecture, the same pottery, the same style of cylinder seals. Although each city was probably politically independent from the others, they shared a culture. It seems that their inhabitants spoke the same language, and they recognized the powers of one another's city gods.

The documents they wrote show that at least some of them interacted peaceably with one another.

Historians refer to their era, from around 3500 to 2900 BCE, as the Uruk period. The urban way of life in Uruk, with its huge buildings, high officials, social hierarchy, and temple-sponsored crafts-workshops, was almost incomparably more sophisticated than that of the villages and towns that came before, but the Uruk population had descended from those earlier peoples. The changes in technology and architecture were locally grown, not imported, and they were dramatic.

Whereas earlier peoples had manufactured their pottery by hand, adding eye-catching designs and glazes, the Uruk craftsmen mostly produced pottery on the newly invented wheel, rarely adding any adornments. Quantity, now possible with a type of mass production, seems to have taken priority over quality in ceramic manufacture. Metals were worked in much greater amounts than had been true before, with copper (sometimes worked with arsenic to add hardness) used for tools and weapons, and gold and silver for jewelry.

The economic records show that the making of cloth was a large-scale enterprise, probably sponsored by the temple of Inanna. To judge from images on cylinder seals, men were employed in herding and sheering (or plucking) the sheep, while women did the spinning and weaving. This was certainly true in later Mesopotamian history. Women's work was, in this way, always central to the economy.

Surprisingly, Uruk-style buildings, pottery, and tools have also been excavated far from southern Mesopotamia, in Syria, Anatolia, and Iran. These telltale artifacts show that the people who created them had traveled, deliberately, from southern Mesopotamia in order to set up new colonies in distant lands. Some of the colonists went to existing towns and created their own neighborhoods there, living alongside the local people but leaving evidence of their presence in the objects they used and the buildings they constructed. Others perhaps attacked foreign towns and took them over violently, settling there and introducing new styles of objects (and presumably new ideas, languages, and organizations). A third group of colonists from the south found unoccupied lands, often at the intersection of a trade route and a river (at a place where it was easily crossed), and set up new cities in the virgin territory. These cities, such as Habuba Kabira in Syria, look a lot like Uruk (the people even used the same beveled-rim bowls for rations) but with more evidence of urban planning.

The areas the Uruk people colonized were not previously "uncivilized"—they had their own histories of development, with farming and towns and craftsmanship. Indeed, the very fact that these lands were growing more sophisticated might have drawn the Uruk colonists to them. The peoples there had access to goods that the southerners needed or wanted, such as metal ores and flint for tools or timber for construction. One theory is that each of the colonies was formed by a different southern Mesopotamian city, each trying to outdo its neighbors in the acquisition of luxury goods and the control of trade.

No matter the reasons behind it, what has been referred to as the "Uruk phenomenon" or the "urban revolution" was like an explosion across the Near East. Brilliant thinkers, explorers, and inventors, whose names are completely unknown to us, built up a whole complex of interwoven technologies and institutions—including cities, government, writing, monumental architecture, the wheel, and bronze working—and set them rolling toward the future, which took them up avidly. The (also unknown) leaders corralled their greatest resource—manpower—and organized it. Men built temples, dug canals, farmed fields, herded animals, and smelted metal ore. Women spun and wove cloth, and probably brewed beer and made pottery. They were all "paid" with some of the goods that the state or temple produced (beer, bread, and wool).

Other men and women went off to distant lands and set up smaller versions of Uruk, certainly keeping in touch with home through messengers, and presumably sending goods that could be useful to their mother cities. Other men learned to write in the proto-cuneiform script in order to keep track of at least some of this activity. Yet others developed the skills to carve intricate cylinder seals used by members of the elite to identify their goods.

Was there any private economic activity in the Uruk period at all? If there was, it would not show up in the proto-cuneiform documents, which record only what was relevant to the temples. Were the priests authoritarian figures, remote and feared? Or were they more accessible, spiritual leaders, followed because of their connection to the gods? There is no way to know. Their names do not even appear in the written record. Not until a few centuries later, around 2900 BCE, did their successors build palaces and begin to rule as kings.

One wonders also if the people of Uruk were aware of just how technologically and economically advanced their civilization was becoming. Were they aware of people in villages not so far away, or not so long before, who had experienced life so differently? Did they think of themselves as being on what we might call the "cutting edge"? Obviously they could not imagine that theirs was the first of countless cities to come, could not foresee that the memory aid system they had invented would evolve into a writing system capable of recording any spoken word or thought. We think of this era as revolutionary. But did they?

Chapter 3
The Early Dynastic period, 2900–2334 BCE

Around 2900 BCE, hereditary kingship developed in Mesopotamia as—to the minds of the people—the best way to administer a region and its population. Once kingship had been invented (not just here but in many places and times around the world), this institution wrapped itself so securely and intimately around the concept of power and statehood that a state without a king was an anomaly, right up to very recent times.

Kingship seemed so obvious and right to the Mesopotamians that they believed that it had been invented by the gods, that it had come "down from heaven." Some later scribes made a grand list of all the kings from the beginning of time to their own era. They called it "When kingship came down from heaven," which was its first line. To modern scholars it is the Sumerian King List. It was far from accurate, awarding early kings reigns that were tens of thousands of years long, rewriting history so that all of Mesopotamia was always ruled from one city at a time, with various cities successively taking power from one another, and forgetting some dynasties altogether. But, for all its faults, the Sumerian King List shows how important kingship was to the Mesopotamians, and how much they wished that their history had followed a regular pattern. The Mesopotamians were fond of order. It reassured them that the proper gods were in control of the universe.

The gods wanted people to be ruled by kings; that was another message of the Sumerian King List. It was not just a convenient fiction invented by the kings themselves, or by the scribes who created the list; it seems to have been a universally held belief. Even the gods themselves had a king—the great god Enlil, who lived in the city of Nippur. According to Mesopotamian belief, at some impossibly remote time in the past, before kingship had come down from heaven, the gods had lived on the earth and in the skies all by themselves. They did, however, need food, drink, and shelter, and Enlil, as king, needed these most of all.

Lesser gods had therefore been forced to work in Enlil's fields, but they had grown tired of the backbreaking labor. They put down their tools and threatened to revolt. Someone else should be forced to do this work, they decided. So an enterprising god came up with the bright idea of creating humans. These would be god-shaped creatures, with the same faces, bodies, emotions, relationships, and language as the gods (who, of course, spoke the local language, Sumerian), but, unlike the gods, they would be powerless and would die after just a short time on earth. Enlil and the other gods could insist that humans do their bidding—plant and plow their fields, make their food, build their shrines and decorate them with the most expensive and rare materials like gold and silver, weave fine clothes for them, pray to them, sing hymns to them—and the humans could never rebel. The gods held all the cards.

This, at least, was what the Mesopotamians believed around a millennium after kingship developed, when the myth was written down, and it seems likely that it was already the common belief when kingship first developed, the era known as the Early Dynastic period. Perhaps it had even been believed during the Uruk period. Every human alive, the king included, was just a servant to the gods, and those gods could choose to treat him or her however they wanted. If the gods were well cared for, they might be merciful, even generous. Harvests could be plentiful, flocks could expand, people could be healthy, women could bear many children, men could be victorious in war. If the gods were angry, though, or just annoyed, they could do inconceivable damage.

The realm of the gods closely resembled that of the humans, not just in having a king and in living in houses (their temples) and needing food and drink and company. They also married and had children. They quarreled and loved and lied. There was a hierarchy among them, with some gods serving others. None of them could claim to know everything or see everything or to be infinitely wise. Unlike humans, though, they did not die, and they had immense power. Among them, they ran the world, but any one of them had limits on his or her dominion. They needed one another, just as humans do.

Order was maintained in the universe because the king of the gods possessed an object called the "Tablet of Destinies" on which were inscribed the *me* (pronounced "may"). These *me* were never written down on any earthly tablet, as far as we know, for human edification. But they encompassed all that kept chaos at bay. Humans were not significant enough, in the Mesopotamian view, to have any major role in cosmic events. It was neither here nor there to the gods what humans actually believed about them. They simply were. And just as the gods needed a king, so too did the humans. This was part of the cosmic order.

Scholars are unsure of how hereditary kingship really developed. Perhaps powerful war leaders were able to convince their armies to keep them in power even when not at war. Perhaps a council of elders appointed a secular leader to balance the power of the priests. And just as professions tended to run in families, the king might have trained his son in the arts of leadership, grooming him for the throne. Who better for the gods to choose as a new king than someone who had spent his childhood at the side of the old king? The Sumerian term for king, "lugal," literally meant "big man."

The city-state of Lagash

Mesopotamia was not unified during the Early Dynastic period. Each of the major cities was in the hands of a king who also controlled the area around the city, including farmland, villages, and sometimes lesser cities. Each of these city-states was home to a patron god or goddess, who lived in the main temple. The people living in the city-states shared a belief in one another's gods; after all, these gods were related to one another. But that did not mean that the city-states always got along. Alliances could quickly disintegrate into animosities and armed confrontations. One city-state is particularly well known for this; this was Lagash (modern Al Hiba in Iraq), home to the god Ningirsu and to a dynasty of kings who squabbled for generations with their counterparts in the neighboring city-state of Umma.

4. In this relief sculpture, the hands of King Enannatum of Lagash are folded in prayer. His exaggerated facial features are typical of Sumerian art of this time.

A stone tablet, engraved with a royal inscription of Enannatum, one of the kings of Lagash, provides evidence of the way in which religion and kingship were inextricably entwined. The tablet was found by archaeologists in the foundations of the temple of Inanna in Lagash, called the Ibgal. This extensive complex was oval in shape, as were many Early Dynastic temples in other cities, with a large courtyard and a platform on which Inanna's temple was constructed. It was not at the center of the city; for some reason, Inanna's home was at the southwestern edge. The tablet was carefully enclosed in a box along with a copper statuette representing Enannatum's personal god, Shulutula. Votive gifts like this were crucial to the construction of a new temple. Several were found in the foundations of each structure, almost always with a stone tablet and a statuette together, always hidden away from view.

The inscription begins with a dedication to the goddess, a list of the king's connections to the gods, and a genealogy, relating him to former kings:

> For Inanna, goddess of all the lands, Enannatum, the king of (the city-state of) Lagash . . ., the great governor for (the god) Ningirsu, the one given a good name by Inanna, . . . the son of Akurgal, the king of Lagash, the beloved brother of Eannatum, the king of Lagash—

It continues by describing the construction of the Ibgal, the very temple in which the inscription was found:

> For Inanna he constructed (the temple oval) Ibgal; for her he made (the temple precinct) Eanna better (than any other) in all the lands; he furnished it with gold and silver.

The inscription ends by giving the reason for its having been written and placed with the statuette of Enannatum's personal god:

> He put (this) in place so that his god, Shulutula, might pray forever to Inanna in the Ibgal for the well-being of Enannatum, the one with whom Inanna communicates, the king of Lagash.
>
> The king who keeps it permanently in good condition will be my friend.

This inscription includes a great deal more information than did the earlier economic documents from Uruk. The scribe who wrote it, around 2450 BCE, was using the script (now cuneiform, rather than proto-cuneiform) in a very different way from the official who recorded that two sheep had (perhaps) been delivered to the temple of Inanna in Uruk. This later scribe wrote not to keep track of commodities but to express complex thoughts and to commemorate the king's piety and devotion, as reflected in his construction of the goddess's temple.

Early Dynastic cuneiform writing

The scribe was no longer limited to using symbols only for nouns and numbers. The script had developed into an elegant means of expressing all kinds of ideas. It featured a combination of types of signs, some of which still stood for whole words, some for phonetic sounds, and some for so-called determinatives, signs that were not read aloud but that helped the reader know which category a word fell into (such as a symbol used for wooden objects, or one that indicated gods' names, or one for city names). An unintended outcome of this greater complexity is that scholars can identify the language behind the script as Sumerian. (This was an impossibility for texts from the Uruk period.) The scribes did not, however, try to express every part of speech; their script was still a shorthand version of language. Sometimes they would choose to conjugate a verb appropriately; often they would not.

To add to the complications of reading texts from this era, Sumerian was not the only language spoken in southern

Mesopotamia (the region known as Sumer). Akkadian, the Semitic language of central Mesopotamia, showed up in subtle ways as well. Some words in Sumerian had been borrowed from Akkadian. Some scribes had Akkadian names even though they wrote in Sumerian, which suggests that they were bilingual.

In the Early Dynastic period writing was not yet being used for many of what we would think of as its obvious purposes. It was still fundamentally utilitarian. The kings had, however, begun to realize its potential for extending communication, in an almost magical way, beyond what could be accomplished with the spoken word. Writing could perpetually and eternally address an audience on a king's behalf; the words were always there, even when the king was not thinking about them. Given that the population was almost entirely illiterate, such an audience was mostly made up of gods. The statuette of the king's personal god (or sometimes of the king himself), inscribed with the same text as the tablet, could therefore pray continuously in a way that a real person could not. (Just as the statue of Enannatum's personal god in the foundation deposit was described as praying constantly to the much more powerful Inanna.) Writing could also address an audience even after its author had died—an audience of those as-yet-unborn kings who might uncover the tablet and statuette when remodeling or rebuilding the temple at some distant future time. As Enannatum noted, "The king who keeps it permanently in good condition will be my friend."

Although many of the writings by Early Dynastic kings were created for the dedication of temples to the gods, some recounted the kings' other great deeds, such as victories in battle (organized military forces having been one of the products of the urban revolution). These victories, too, were usually credited to the gods, by whom the king had been "chosen in the heart," and "given a good name." Such inscriptions also, like the foundation text by Enannatum, almost always listed the name of the king's predecessor—his father or brother who had served as king before him. He truly had a right to the throne, he asserted, having been selected by the gods and born into the royal line.

Some aspects of the culture had changed little since the end of the Uruk period, six hundred years before. The inscription shows that Inanna still needed temples and that she required offerings. King Enannatum gave her more than just food and drink; he claimed that he furnished her temple with expensive and showy gold and silver. And the king also interceded with the gods for his people. As Enannatum put it, he was "the one with whom Inanna communicates." He hoped, in exchange, that she would provide for his "well-being." Theirs was a complex and interdependent relationship. The same might have been true of the earlier priests of Uruk, but they had not yet developed a writing system that could have expressed such longings.

Temple and palace estates

The major Early Dynastic temples, such as that of Inanna, all owned extensive estates—fields, orchards, herds of animals, workshops—as did the palaces. It was not only the king who had a royal palace; in the kingdom of Lagash so did his queen. In fact all of the 1,700 administrative tablets that were found at the later capital of Lagash, called Girsu, came from the queen's palace. The queen personally administered its estate. (Excavators have not found the king's palace.)

Not far from the Ibgal temple of Inanna where the dedicatory tablet was found, archaeologists excavated the earliest known brewery anywhere in Mesopotamia (a tablet found there even mentioned the brewer). Its main oven, five meters across, completely filled a large room. Another court housed a large tank and several ovens. The temple must have produced tremendous quantities of beer, not just for the god himself but also presumably for the rations of his many servants and workers. Barley beer was the staple drink of all Mesopotamians, being both nutritious and less germ-filled than river water. The various palaces and temples probably produced similarly vast quantities of food and textiles. Writing continued to be essential to keep track of it all. Many, perhaps most, of the inhabitants of each city-state presumably worked for a temple or palace as farmers, herdsmen, or artisans of various kinds.

Battles between Umma and Lagash

A series of texts from Lagash records a continuous struggle with the neighboring kingdom of Umma, to the west. The two states fought for generations over a broad swath of land that separated them. Some of the inscriptions included surprising amounts of detail. Enannatum's brother and predecessor, the similarly named King Eannatum, described an injury that he received in battle and the pain it caused him: "A person shot an arrow at Eannatum. He was shot through by the arrow and had difficult moving. He cried out in the face of it."

Some of these documents about the conflict were written on stone monuments, which perhaps were placed as physical markers right on the border between the two kingdoms. Again, the kings sometimes wrote to future kings in these inscriptions, attempting to control their actions. They worried that their successors might obliterate the good works they had achieved. One king wrote about (and on) such a monument: "If another leader destroys it there, or takes it away and makes off (with it), may his city, like a place (infested) with harmful snakes, not allow him to hold his head erect. May poisonous fangs bite that ruler in his ruined palace!"

At around the same time that they invented inscriptions by which to communicate with gods and with future kings, the kings' scribes began to use writing for addressing those at a different kind of distance from themselves—kings of other lands. The first letters ever written seem to have been sent from one king to another, carried by messengers. Sometimes the letters bore peaceful tidings and were accompanied by gifts; at other times a letter could remind its recipient of past alliances or animosities. Some letters might even have threatened war. One king of Lagash sent a fierce message to Umma: "Be it known that your city will be completely destroyed! Surrender! Be it kno[wn] that Umma will be completely destroyed!" The original does not survive; it was quoted in an inscription. It is interesting to note from this that messengers traveled to Umma even when relations between the two kingdoms were obviously extremely hostile. Note also that the king of Lagash felt the necessity of warning the king of Umma that he would be attacked. Earlier messengers had certainly recited communications from memory, but a written letter could serve both as a memory aid to the messenger and as concrete evidence of the sender's intentions when checked by the recipient's scribe.

People living in the cities of Girsu and Lagash, or in the many villages within the kingdom, did not necessarily think of themselves as Sumerian, even though Sumerian culture was fairly uniform across southern Mesopotamia. Their allegiance was to their city-state; this was reinforced by their frequent wars with their neighbors. Lagash and Umma were, in turn, surrounded by a number of other city-state kingdoms, including Uruk and Ur to the south, some of which were friendly, others hostile. To the north of Sumer, a much larger kingdom, Kish, dominated the region later known as Akkad. The king of Kish even sometimes enforced order in Sumer. For example, Enannatum's son, Enmetena, wrote that the border between Lagash and Umma had been determined by the great god Enlil himself and had been confirmed by the king of Kish: "Mesalim, king of Kish, at the command of (the god) Ishtaran, measured the field and set up a (boundary-) stone there." The authority of the king of Kish was therefore acknowledged, at least temporarily, by both the king of Umma and the king of Lagash.

Sometimes, Sumerian kings managed to conquer other cities, inspiring them to assert that they, too, could take the title "King of Kish" (though it is unlikely that they actually controlled Kish itself). Eannatum of Lagash, the brother of Enannatum, claimed this title. So did a king of Uruk who conquered neighboring Ur and then signed on to a treaty of "brotherhood"—alliance—with King Enmetena of Lagash.

This was not the first time that Ur had been conquered; earlier documents record its defeat by Lagash. One might conclude from this that Ur was a weak, minor kingdom at this time. In fact, the opposite seems to have been true.

The royal tombs of Ur

Although not much of the Early Dynastic city of Ur has been excavated, in the 1920s archaeologists uncovered there a huge cemetery of about two thousand graves. Many of these contained the bodies of wealthy citizens, and sixteen of them captured the imagination not only of the excavator, Sir Leonard Woolley, but of people around the world. Each of the sixteen graves included a subterranean tomb building surrounded by a burial pit. The tomb housed the body of an elite man or woman, along with innumerable objects for his or her afterlife—metal bowls, musical instruments, jewelry, sculptures, weapons, furniture, food, even cosmetics. Were they all kings and queens? Woolley thought so. More recent scholars are not so sure; perhaps some of them were priests and priestesses.

In any event, they were people of immense wealth. Many of the luxurious objects buried with them were of gold, silver, copper, and semiprecious stones, none of which could be found natively anywhere near Ur. The raw materials had been imported by the leaders of Ur from as far away as the Indus Valley and Afghanistan. Over months and years these materials had been worked into exquisite objects by highly skilled craftsmen, only to be buried for the continued use of the leader in the afterlife. Even today the objects from the so-called royal tombs attract huge crowds when exhibited in museums.

Another aspect of the royal tombs was more disturbing. Woolley himself described one tomb:

> The pit was roughly rectangular . . . and was approached as usual by a sloped ramp. In it lay the bodies of six men-servants and sixty-eight women; the men lay along the side by the door, the bodies of the women were disposed in regular rows across the floor, every one lying on her side with legs slightly bent and hands brought up near the face, so close together that the heads of those in one row rested on the legs of those in the row above.

These were not the bodies of kings or queens but of men and women who had been sacrificed in order to be buried with their lord or lady. Woolley believed they had died without a struggle—perhaps poisoned—but recent studies of a few skulls show that at least some of the attendants were killed by a blow to the head. Were the attendants terrorized into submission, or did they agree willingly to end their lives this way? The women were dressed in finery to match their dead mistress, with "red coats with beaded cuffs and shell-ring belts, head-dresses of gold or silver, great lunate ear-rings and multiple necklaces of blue and gold."

Presumably the attendants and the wealth were interred so as to be available in the afterlife to the leaders who had died. Surprisingly, though, the Mesopotamians rarely wrote about the afterlife. Literary descriptions suggest that the netherworld was a gloomy place—dark, with bad food, and no way out—and there was little about it that suggested either a reward or punishment. It simply existed. And yet, since these kings (and many commoners whose burials also contained gifts and food) took their worldly possessions with them, perhaps they believed that they could improve their lot in the afterlife.

The Early Dynastic kings would not have viewed their kingdoms as small; they had no way of knowing that larger kingdoms were soon to come. Each of them, whether he ruled in Ur, Uruk, Lagash,

Umma, or any of the other states, would have been self-important and perhaps somewhat terrifying to his people. He had the support of the gods; he could command soldiers to fight for him and attendants to die with him. He killed enemies and enforced obedience. Many of his subjects worked in the textile workshops, breweries, kitchens, fields, and orchards of his palace. But in return he provided for them. A favorite image that kings chose for themselves in statues from the Early Dynastic period shows the monarch with a basket of earth for construction on his head. He might be a mighty ruler, but he was also a builder, erecting monuments to his gods and taking care of his people.

Chapter 4
The Akkadian Empire, 2334–2193 BCE

In the mid-twenty-fourth century BCE, a new type of state emerged in Mesopotamia, one that incorporated dozens of former kingdoms. Whereas earlier kings had managed to bring at most a few city-states together through conquest or treaty, an upstart leader named Sargon was able to conquer almost all of what is now Iraq along with much of Syria—he forged the world's first empire. Sargon probably began life as a commoner, overthrew the king of Kish, and became, in his own immodest words, one "to whom Enlil has given no rival; to him he (Enlil) gave the Upper and Lower Sea (the Mediterranean and Persian Gulf)."

These words come from an inscription that Sargon commissioned to commemorate his victories. Although the original version of it is lost, the words are still preserved. This is because, not long after Sargon's time, a meticulous scribe made a copy of all the royal inscriptions to be found in the main temple to Enlil, in the city of Nippur. He wrote them all out on a large clay tablet and included Sargon's words among them. The scribe's version was then copied again centuries later. The Mesopotamians had a fascination with the past and a surprisingly sophisticated understanding of the value of copying ancient documents accurately and preserving them for the future.

Sargon's campaigns were almost certainly relentless and brutal. He attacked Uruk, which had been the site, nine centuries before, of the elaborate temple to Inanna with its dazzling mosaic walls. He claimed that he "vanquished Uruk in battle and smote fifty governors and the city." Then he had turned to Ur, home to the fabulously rich leaders who had taken dozens of attendants with them to their deaths. Again he "vanquished Ur in battle and smote the city and destroyed its fortress." One city after another fell to his armies, Lagash and Umma among them. These former enemies now paid their taxes and tribute to the same overlord. Having reached the Persian Gulf, with no further Sumerian cities to conquer, Sargon, with great symbolism "washed his weapons in the sea."

In addition to his southern conquests, Sargon marched north and conquered perhaps as far as the Mediterranean. Across the empire he demoted local rulers and placed Akkadian-speaking officials in charge, transforming the traditional city-state structure that had developed over centuries. (Akkadian, Sargon's native tongue, was the Semitic language spoken in central Mesopotamia.) Rebellions repeatedly broke out, not just during his reign but in those of his successors as well. But Sargon hung on tenaciously to his empire.

After repeated victories, Sargon's attention turned back toward his home. He wrote that he "restored the territory of Kish." Kish had dominated the region of Akkad for centuries, and it was perhaps Sargon's original home, so he was keen to build it up and to restore and remodel it, rather than to destroy its walls as he had in southern cities. But he did not set up his capital there. Instead he built a new city, called Akkad or Agade, which gained a reputation for immense wealth and luxury. Regrettably, archaeologists have not yet identified which of the ancient sites was the location of Akkad, though it probably lay to the east of Kish on the Tigris River. Its palaces and temples, houses and archives await discovery by future generations of scholars.

Besides a few copies of inscriptions, not much is therefore preserved from Sargon's own time. The few contemporary documents that survive suggest that Sargon wanted to portray himself as—and indeed to be—something quite different from the kings who came before him. He did not initially use the traditional title "King of Kish" that previous kings had aspired to. Not that he did not rule Kish; he did, and he could have used the title without exaggeration. But he chose to be "King of Akkad" instead.

Sargon also seems to have taken land away from some of the temples in order to control it himself, and to have allowed some of it to be acquired by private individuals. Such land could be bought and sold, which might have been an innovation. He also called upon a group of 5,400 men and put them into roles that gave them a special relationship to him. He noted that he fed them daily; they were almost certainly some sort of elite military force, supported from the wealth of the king's estates.

In one of his inscriptions, Sargon boasted of close ties that he had forged with distant lands: Dilmun (Bahrain), Magan (Oman), and Meluhha (the Indus Valley). He claimed that boats from these lands came all the way to Akkad with their wares. Archaeological finds confirm that the Mesopotamians were indeed in contact with those regions at this time; luxury goods made of carnelian, diorite, copper, and lapis lazuli have been excavated from Akkadian levels at Mesopotamian sites. These materials would have arrived on the foreign boats.

More than any previous king, Sargon seems to have focused his attention outward from his local area onto distant places, using conquest, trade, and diplomacy to put his stamp on the world of his time. At least within his empire, this meant that resources from great distances were funneled in to Akkad, to the benefit of the capital and the detriment of the conquered lands.

All of this extraction of wealth must have infuriated his vanquished subjects. One would think that they would have told their children and grandchildren stories of their oppression and of the cruelty and villainy of Sargon. But those were not the stories that survived. Sargon was certainly remembered but not as a brutal tyrant. Ultimately he was viewed as a hero. Over time his life story gained mythical touches: he was born in secret, he miraculously survived being cast off down a river in a basket, he was loved by the goddess Ishtar (the Akkadian name for Inanna), and so on. His was a life to idolize and, for kings, to emulate. More than fifteen hundred years after his death, the stories of Sargon's deeds continued to be told.

Enheduanna, priestess of the moon god

One reason for Sargon's propaganda success, perhaps, was his use of religion to legitimize his reign. Not only did he claim that the gods gave him his empire (just as the earlier Sumerian kings had claimed that their local gods chose them for kingship), he also placed his daughter in one of the highest religious positions in all of Mesopotamia: she became the high priestess of the moon god Nanna in the city of Ur, where the god had his chief residence. No doubt the kings and queens, or priests and priestesses who had been buried in the sumptuous tombs in the Early Dynastic period, and who lay just meters away from Nanna's temple, had also been devoted to the moon god.

The daughter's name was Enheduanna; she might have been given this Sumerian name at the time of her appointment (her native tongue, like that of her father, was Akkadian). In placing Enheduanna in an eminent position in Ur, Sargon perhaps hoped to convince the people there that he had their interests in mind. He probably also benefited from the appointment in that Enheduanna took control of the immense estate associated with Nanna's temple and, with it, a good part of the economy of Ur. His motives, however, would not only have been political and economic. Although Sargon's dynasty was dedicated to Inanna/Ishtar, he also wanted the support of the moon god Nanna (also known as Ashimbabbar).

Enheduanna had some of the same responsibilities as a governor: she represented the king in a conquered city, and she administered extensive lands and a large workforce. But as priestess she also played a religious role, and in that role she composed hymns to the gods.

> I, Enheduanna the *en* priestess, entered my holy *gipar* (palace) in your service.
> I carried the ritual basket, and intoned the song of joy. . . .
> The woman (Inanna) . . .; foreign lands and flood lands lie at her feet.
> The woman (Inanna) too is exalted, and can make cities tremble. . . .
> I, Enheduanna, will recite a prayer to you. To you, holy Inanna, I shall give free vent to my tears like sweet beer! . . .
> Do not be anxious about Ashimbabbar.

These words come from a hymn of 153 lines. As in the royal inscription written by Enannatum of Lagash 150 years before, the goddess Inanna takes center stage. Like Enannatum, Enheduanna describes bringing gifts to the goddess (the ritual basket and a prayer). But, unlike in a royal inscription, Enheduanna did not put the emphasis on herself and her deeds. Instead, it was the goddess who was "exalted."

Enheduanna wrote two other hymns as well; like this one they are beautifully composed, full of emotion and vivid imagery. They are sometimes referred to as the first literary works for which we know the author, and therefore Enheduanna herself gets named as the first author in the world to take credit for a composition. But it is a subtle distinction; as far as we know Enheduanna did not suddenly come up with the idea of authorship. She might well have included her name for the same reasons that a king named himself in a royal inscription, and there were plenty of precedents for that. Enheduanna was familiar with hymns because of her religious role, and she was familiar with royal inscriptions because Sargon, her father, was the king. Our modern definition of the hymn as literature in contrast to a royal inscription as propaganda would probably have been lost on her.

The most surprising aspect of the hymn, which she wrote with such passion, is that she was the high priestess of Nanna/ Ashimbabbar, not of Inanna, although it was the latter to whom she addressed her words. Enheduanna here was following her father's lead. Sargon's devotion to Inanna/Ishtar is evident in his inscription. Ishtar was the first deity that he mentioned, with Sargon named as the "overseer" who worked on her behalf: "Sargon, king of Akkad, overseer of Ishtar, king of Kish, anointed priest of (the god) Anu, king of the country, great *ensi* of Enlil." These other gods, Anu and Enlil, were important to include because Anu was seen as the original father of the gods, and Enlil (Anu's son) was the king of the gods and had been traditionally the god most connected with earthly kings. Sargon claimed to have the support of all three. His successes were their successes. Enheduanna recognized her joint (and perhaps conflicting) loyalties to Nanna and Inanna in her hymn. "Do not be anxious about Ashimbabbar," she wrote to the goddess.

Enheduanna alluded vaguely to a crisis in Ur, her adopted home. She wrote in another part of the hymn that "My Nanna has paid no heed to me. He has destroyed me utterly." Some scholars think that perhaps the disaster she suffered was shared by all of the people of Ur, and that the city had been attacked by Uruk. Or perhaps her crisis was more personal.

Enheduanna expected the moon god, to whom she was formally dedicated, to have saved her, but he did not. It seems that she was even denied her position as priestess and was sent into exile: "He (Nanna) stood there in triumph and drove me out of the temple. He made me fly like a swallow from the window. . . . He stripped me of the rightful crown of the *en* priestess." Her appeal to Inanna was the desperate move of a woman who felt that her god had abandoned her. Hence the acts mentioned in the hymn—the greetings, gifts, prayers, songs, and tears to Inanna, along with the hymn itself. An ancient editorial comment at the end of the hymn notes that it had its desired effect: "The powerful lady (Inanna) . . .

has accepted her offerings from her. Inanna's holy heart has been assuaged."

The city-state of Ebla

The northern kingdoms that Sargon had conquered were larger than their Sumerian counterparts. He boasted of having been given the Syrian lands of Mari and Ebla by their local god. When archaeologists identified the sites that were home to these ancient cities (Mari was on the Euphrates at Tell Hariri, Ebla farther north and west at Tell Mardikh), they found evidence of impressive Early Dynastic communities surrounded by extensive kingdoms.

The discoveries of these Syrian kingdoms came long after the excavations of the Sumerian city-states. Historians and archaeologists had concluded that civilization had developed in Sumer and that surrounding areas were less advanced, so cities like Ebla and Mari were initially thought by many to have been peripheral and dependent for their inspiration on the south. In recent years, though, scholars have seen the northern kingdoms as having made important contributions of their own.

The kings of Ebla and Mari squabbled and reconciled, drew up peace treaties and broke them, just like the southern kings of the Early Dynastic period. They may in fact have been more sophisticated in diplomatic affairs than were their southern counterparts. Although none of the royal inscriptions from Ebla and Mari survive for this period, administrative documents recording goods going in and out of the palace show that men known as stewards were in charge of diplomatic contacts between the two kingdoms. Traveling from one city to the other took the stewards about two weeks, and they made the journey repeatedly. They carried with them gifts from Mari to Ebla (often in the form of lapis lazuli) and from Ebla to Mari (often silver). The stewards also received personal gifts of silver from the courts they visited. Other stewards traveled even farther; a letter survives from

Ebla that was addressed to an ambassador from Hamazi—a city probably in northern Mesopotamia. The two powers exchanged valuable gifts and letters. Kings of Ebla also arranged marriages for their daughters to distant kings.

Economic records show that staggering amounts of silver and gold changed hands between Ebla and Mari. In fact, given that Ebla is located nowhere near a gold mine and that it was a kingdom of only about two hundred thousand people, the amount of gold in use there is almost unbelievable. One administrative text accounts for the gold used in the manufacture of an enormous jar: "Total: 838.20 minas of gold for one jar," with a listing of the amounts of gold used in different parts of the jar, including its base, stand, shoulder, and lip. The equivalent of 838 minas is 394 kilograms (869 pounds) of gold. (At a recent rate of $1,500 per ounce, such a jar would be worth almost $20.1 million if made today.) A number of such ceremonial jars were made, in varying sizes. None of them has been found, of course. They would have been melted down long ago, perhaps even by Sargon when he brought Ebla into his empire. The riches found in the royal tombs of Ur would have been small change in comparison.

The records of the gold jars, and of all other parts of the Ebla economy, were written on clay tablets in the cuneiform script, as in Sumer. The scribes of Ebla used the Sumerian language for some of their texts, clearly having been taught the script originally by southern teachers, but they also used cuneiform in order to write in their native Semitic language, known as Eblaite. Thousands of the tablets, beautifully laid out and elegantly written, were recovered from an archive room in the palace where they had been carefully stored on shelves. The surfaces of the large tablets were divided into hundreds of rectangles in what almost looks like a checkerboard pattern. Each rectangular section contained a number of cuneiform signs representing a word or a phrase. The scribes wrote these sections in columns, to be read from top to bottom of the tablet. Although most of the tablets recorded details of the administration of the kingdom, some of them were used by scribes in the course of their education or as reference works—lists of words in Sumerian, just like the ones that had been used as long ago as the Uruk period. Some of the lists gave the Eblaite equivalents of Sumerian terms (these were helpful not just to Eblaite-speaking scribes but to modern scholars deciphering the ancient languages).

Akkadian innovations

Sargon's grandson, King Naram-Sin, also claimed to have conquered Ebla and even said that he was the first to do so. Perhaps this was hyperbole: the kingdom might have rebelled after Sargon's death and achieved some independence, only to be brought back under Akkadian rule. Or perhaps the city had capitulated to Sargon without a fight when he conquered Mari so that Naram-Sin's conquest was indeed a first. Naram-Sin was so convinced of his own exalted status that he had himself deified (or, according to legend, acquiesced when his people chose to make him a god)—he was one of the very few Mesopotamian kings to do so. A well-known image of Naram-Sin from a large stela produced during his reign shows him striding heroically up a mountainside, weapons in hand, dead enemies underfoot, and horns on his helmet. Only gods wore horned helmets.

It was a time of innovation in many ways. Not only did Sargon conceive of and build a vast empire, he also came up with ways to organize and control the territories he had conquered. He enriched the state and himself in various ways. And he and his successors promoted a spirit of experimentation among artisans and craftsmen. Objects found in archaeological contexts from the era of the Akkadian empire are often eye-catching. Cylinder seals featured a wide range of subjects, carved with a skill and subtlety rarely matched in later Mesopotamian history. A copper head of a king of Akkad (it is unclear which one) is much more lifelike than Early Dynastic sculptures of kings, with their exaggerated

5. A detail of a relief sculpture from the victory stela of King Naram-Sin of Akkad shows the king wearing a horned crown, which denotes his status as a god, and carrying a bow.

features and huge staring eyes. The stela of Naram-Sin conquering his enemies was the work of an innovative (though anonymous) artist who broke free of the usual register lines that had divided up Early Dynastic art into horizontal scenes. His figures climb the mountain and fall from it in organized abandon.

But who was Sargon? Where did he come from (given that the legend about the basket on a river is highly suspect)? How did he administer his far-flung empire from day to day? Few originals of his inscriptions survive, and those only in fragments. There are no administrative documents dated to his reign, no letters to his governors or to foreign kings. We do not even have an image of him sculpted during his lifetime.

When the site of Akkad is eventually found, perhaps much more will be learned about Sargon and this first dynasty of emperors. For now they remain somewhat enigmatic. Sargon cast a long shadow over the centuries that followed, as kings from many lands tried to replicate his military successes. But in a way he is missing from his own portrait, a hero without a face or voice.

Chapter 5
The Third Dynasty of Ur, 2193–2004 BCE

The Akkadian Empire collapsed after the reign of the fourth successor to Sargon, falling victim to internal rebellions and invasions of highland peoples from the Zagros Mountains. Various kings then split the former empire among them, each having power over a limited area. One of these kings, Gudea, who ruled Lagash in the twenty-second century BCE, continued Sargon's practice of importing luxury goods from Magan (Oman) and Dilmun (Bahrain). His face is familiar to visitors to the Louvre, the British Museum, the Metropolitan Museum, and several other museums because of the many diorite statues of himself that he dedicated to the gods, which are now in those museums' collections. But Gudea's kingdom was dwarfed in size and influence by that of the Third Dynasty of Ur, created by a king named Ur-Namma.

Ur-Namma started his life as a subject of the king of Uruk, but around 2112 BCE he seized power in Ur and united much of what is now Iraq under his rule, though he did not manage to conquer as far to the north as Sargon had done. But rather than describing his conquests as violent affairs, he referred to "liberating" the lands from their former overlords. He presented himself as a king who had the welfare of his people uppermost in his thoughts.

Ur-Namma also was the first king known to have put laws in writing. The laws were probably originally inscribed on a stone stela, but all that survives of them are copies on three broken clay tablets. Unfortunately, only thirty-seven of the laws appear on these tablet fragments; there must have been more.

The prologue to the laws depicts Ur-Namma as a kind, pious king, devoted to order and justice. It begins with the king's epithets "Ur-Namma, the mighty warrior, king of the city of Ur, king of the lands of Sumer and Akkad." Although he could not claim to have inherited the throne, the king referred to himself as "Ur-Namma, son born of the goddess Ninsun" as though his mother had been a goddess. The patron god of Ur, Nanna, also figured prominently in the prologue to the laws. The god Nanna was said to have received "the kingship of the city of Ur" from the ancestral gods An and Enlil. The earthly kings of Ur were beholden to Nanna, just as priestess Enheduanna had been, two centuries earlier.

Ur-Namma's conquests are mentioned only briefly in the prologue: "At that time, by the might of Nanna, my lord, I liberated . . . whatever (territories) were under the subjugation of Anshan." Instead, he emphasizes the ways in which he standardized weights and measures, including "I made the copper *bariga*-measure and standardized it at 60 silas." Most importantly, he asserts that he protected the weak in society: "I did not deliver the orphan to the rich. I did not deliver the widow to the mighty. I did not deliver the man with but one shekel to the man with one mina (60 shekels). . . . I eliminated enmity, violence, and cries for justice. I established justice in the land."

Ziggurat construction

Ur-Namma also tried endearing himself to his new subjects (and the gods) by sponsoring extensive building projects across the kingdom. At least four cities, including Ur and Uruk, saw the construction of huge solid stepped towers, called ziggurats, dedicated to their local gods. These structures would each have taken hundreds, perhaps thousands, of men to construct.

According to one estimate, the ziggurat in Ur was built of approximately two million baked bricks and five million sun-dried bricks. It has been calculated from the administrative texts of the time that the manufacture and transport of the bricks for just the lower platform of the ziggurat required around 145,700 man-days of work, or 146 days for 1,000 men working together. The texts show that workers were divided into groups of fifty, each with a foreman and five team leaders, one for every ten men. Other workers wove ropes and collected bitumen; others allocated the rations of barley for all the workers; while farmers grew, harvested, and processed the barley.

Meanwhile, scribes recorded all the details. The era of the Third Dynasty of Ur saw an expansion in size and an increase in sophistication of the administrative hierarchies attached to the palaces and temples. Workers on all manner of programs were paid in rations, and officials recorded their names and the amounts they received on clay tablets that were later archived. Because clay tablets could not be added to or changed later, there was no way for scribes to create the equivalent of ledgers. When it came time to create monthly or yearly summaries, the scribes had to copy from dozens or even hundreds of daily account tablets and to add up all the man-hours, along with the totals of incoming and outgoing materials. They organized their annual reports by product, quality, or type of worker, an enormously complicated task. The Mesopotamians craved order in their lives and societies, and this administration was nothing if not orderly—almost obsessively so, it might seem to modern eyes.

Ur-Namma sometimes chose to have himself depicted in artworks, like some of the Early Dynastic kings, with a basket of earth on his head, as though he not only planned and sponsored the construction projects but even worked on the buildings himself. His public image was a far cry from the warlike mien of Akkadian kings such as Sargon or Naram-Sin.

6. This copper alloy figure of King Ur-Namma of Ur with a basket on his head, symbolizing his role as a builder, was part of a foundation deposit for the temple of Inanna in Uruk.

Standardizations

Ur-Namma and his son and successor, Shulgi, made other efforts to unite the land, perhaps recognizing that the people over whom they ruled still thought of themselves more as citizens of a particular city or town than as subjects of a larger kingdom. The prologue to the laws mentions the standardization of all kinds of weights and measures. The kings even standardized brick sizes. The ideal was that plots of land, taxes, and prices across the kingdom would be measured in the same ways and would not need to be converted in order for trade or taxation to take place. The kings were not, however, entirely successful in all aspects of this standardization. Their subjects resisted an attempt to make everyone use the same calendar, for example. Each city had traditionally used unique names for the months, and most of them hung onto these, rather than adopting the month names of the state calendar.

The legal system

The laws themselves were (at least according to the prologue) designed to eliminate "enmity, violence, and cries for justice." People would not take retribution into their own hands but would depend upon the statewide legal system. In writing down the laws, these kings of Ur were not inventing that system. Contracts had existed for centuries, along with courts, judges, and a belief that witnesses and evidence were necessary in order for a just verdict to be determined. The laws that the kings of Ur promulgated were probably legal precedents—memory aids again, reflecting decisions that had previously been made by judges, which could help inform future decisions. Even the complete text of the laws (if we had it) certainly could not have covered all possible crimes and infractions. By writing them down, the kings were doing something similar to what they had done in the foundation inscriptions found in temples: making a permanent record of something that had previously been ephemeral.

The laws were all expressed conditionally. Rather than stating that some particular action was forbidden, each law started with the premise that the infraction might take place and specified an appropriate punishment. For example, a law against false testimony stated that, "If a man presents himself as a witness but is demonstrated to be a perjurer, he shall weigh and deliver 15 shekels of silver." This was a considerable sum; other sources show that one could purchase ten or more unskilled female slaves for that amount. Most punishments, though sometimes financially devastating, did not involve physical harm to the accused. Of the twenty-five laws for which a punishment is preserved in Ur-Namma's collection, twenty (80 percent) resulted in the imposition of a fine or other payment on the condemned man, and one resulted in a physical punishment (having one's mouth scoured with salt). The death penalty was imposed only in four cases, for homicide, rape of a virgin wife of another man, adultery by a married woman, and some other crime pertaining to lawlessness (the meaning of the law is unclear). No one was sent to prison as a penalty for committing a crime.

Witnesses were crucial in the determination of a verdict. Everyone involved in a case had to be willing to swear an oath that he or she was telling the truth. These oaths were deadly serious. Lying under oath was something the gods despised, according to Mesopotamian belief, and the gods could be expected to punish the liar in a much harsher way than did the human judges. If someone was willing to swear an oath, that person's testimony was considered reliable. No one, it was thought, would be crazy enough to lie directly to the gods.

One might assume that judges constituted the primary audience for these laws, that the laws provided practical guidance for actual court cases. That might have been the case, but there is little concrete evidence for it. In the centuries following the time of kings Ur-Namma and Shulgi, laws continued to be disseminated, but no known court records refer specifically to their being consulted. The kings emphasized in the epilogues to their laws (broken, unfortunately, in the case of Ur-Namma) that the laws were part of a program to make "right and truth shine forth" and to bring "well-being to the lands of Sumer and Akkad." Perhaps this did not require that the laws be followed to the letter, only that their spirit be followed.

As with many royal inscriptions, the law collections all concluded with curses against anyone in the future who might deface or destroy the work, anyone who "does anything evil to it, who damages my work, who enters the treasure room, who alters its pedestal, who effaces this inscription and writes his own name (in place of mine), or, because of this curse, induces an outsider to remove it." Over time the curses got longer and more colorful. By the time of the Laws of Hammurabi, more than three hundred years after the reign of Ur-Namma, the curses took up 264 lines of the text and included just about every possible horrible thing that might happen to a king. Each god was addressed individually and asked to create a special kind of terror for any future king who damaged Hammurabi's laws. Inanna, now called Ishtar, was to "strike down his warriors, drench the earth with their blood, make a heap of the corpses of his soldiers upon the plain, . . . and as for him, may she deliver him into the hand of his enemies, and may she lead him bound captive to the land of his enemy."

The kings seem to have been increasingly concerned that their names and deeds not be forgotten. If the curses worked and the stelas survived, then collections of laws, like royal inscriptions, provided insurance against future oblivion. (They were not wrong; here we are still writing about and discussing them, after all.) Some of the kings of Ur even followed in the footsteps of Naram-Sin of Akkad and presented themselves as gods rather than men, to the point of commissioning temples for their own worship.

This is not to say that Ur-Namma and Shulgi were concerned only with their own enduring reputations and did not care about the welfare of their subjects. They seem to have been sincere in their desire for order in the land. They instituted various measures to protect people who might otherwise have been weak or discriminated against—the orphan, widow, and poor "man with but one shekel" of the prologue. They provided for the safety of roads and protected merchants.

Taxation and redistribution

Most dramatically, at least as far as the written record of their era is concerned, they created a system of taxation and redistribution of resources across the kingdom that was remarkable for its complexity and, it seems, efficiency. Approximately 120,000 cuneiform tablets written during the Third Dynasty of Ur have been discovered, and the vast majority of them record details of some component of the immense system created by the kings to process payments, offerings, and compensations.

Many tablets of this kind were drawn up in a place called Puzrish-Dagan, which was created, apparently by King Shulgi, as a clearinghouse for goods—taxes and offerings—that were coming in to the state and going out to the provinces. At least 12,000 cuneiform records are known to have come from Puzrish-Dagan, representing a period of approximately forty years during the Third Dynasty of Ur, starting toward the end of the reign of Shulgi. These documents were the direct successors of the rudimentary economic texts from the Uruk Period. Now, though, a document of this kind included much more information. Nouns could now be qualified with adjectives; also added were the names of the officials involved, other circumstances, and the date when the tablet was drawn up. By now the words were written in lines (rather than in boxes), which were read from left to right, and from top to bottom of the tablet, just as we do in English. Many of the signs represented phonetic sounds, though some still stood for whole words.

A typical administrative tablet from Puzrish-Dagan records some transactions concerning sheep and goats that were sacrificed to the gods. It begins with a list of the sheep and goats to be sacrificed, each one described as "fattened," and designated for a particular god or person:

1 fattened sheep—(for the gods) Enlil, Ninlil
1 fattened sheep—(for the god) Nanna, night-time
4 fattened sheep—Enlil, Ninlil
1 fattened big-goat—Nanna, dawn, when the king entered,
4 fattened sheep—lustration of Nintinugga, via Atu
1 fattened sheep, 1 big-goat—Shulgad, the man of (the land of) Zidahri via Shu-Shulgi, *sukkal* (official).

Next comes the name of the official in charge: "Arad-mu, requisitioner." Then the circumstances of the sacrifice and the source of the animals: "The first day having passed from the month in (the city of) Tummal, expended from the office of (the official) En-dingirmu." The tablet is dated, "Month 8, Year Huhnuri was destroyed" and it ends with a summary: "(Total sheep) 13."

A scribe employed at Puzrish-Dagan would have understood all the implications of this tablet. He would have known to check with the requisitioner, Arad-mu, about any concerns he might have had regarding the transaction. He would have recognized, based on the date, that the sheep and goats listed were for the main annual religious festival in the city of Tummal and that En-dingirmu was the usual official who provided them (he is named on all of the eleven preserved documents of this sort written over an eight-year period). The scribe would have known where, in the complex of buildings at Puzrish-Dagan, to find En-dingirmu, and where to take the sheep, both to the gods and to the man named Shulgad from the distant land of Zidahri. In fact, during the next few days after this document was written, Shulgad received sheep at least five more times. By the fifth day of the month another foreigner had joined him, a man from the land of Harshi. The lands of both

Harshi and Zidahri were in Elam, to the east, beyond the core of the Ur kingdom. These ambassadors were a long way from home, probably visiting Tummal on a diplomatic mission and staying for the festival.

The tablets from Puzrish-Dagan show that it was an unusual place. It might not have had the temples, palaces, and houses of a normal town. Instead, the heart of the city must have been dominated by a complex of buildings dedicated to the management of livestock, including stockyards and slaughterhouses.

Each month, one of the provinces in the kingdom was responsible for sending in its taxes so that wealth was always coming in from somewhere. These taxes were sometimes paid in silver but more often in such goods as barley, flour, reeds, and timber. As much as 48 percent of the barley annually produced in the provinces had to be paid as taxes, which were sent to Puzrish-Dagan and to other major towns. The richer provinces were responsible for supplying the state for more than one month. By spreading the collection of taxes out through the year, the kings assured themselves of regular supplies. The movement of goods was not just a one-way transaction, however. Some provinces took cattle or other livestock away from Puzrish-Dagan, perhaps as repayment for expenses they had incurred on behalf of the state. The river port at Puzrish-Dagan would have been the site of many boats being unloaded, vast quantities of raw materials and animals being recorded by busy scribes. All these goods had to be directed to the right warehouses, and the records of their deliveries had to be filed in the right offices.

But in the case of Puzrish-Dagan, archaeologists have no real sense of the physical spaces in which all this activity took place, because the site has never been formally excavated. Unlike Akkad, this is not because its location is unknown. Puzrish-Dagan is now known as Drehem, a tell ten kilometers southeast of Nippur. Around 1910, documents from Puzrish-Dagan began appearing on the antiquities market in vast quantities, presumably having been dug up by local people. They were purchased by major museums and private collectors and are now spread out across the world. Only recently, with the creation of online projects such as the Cuneiform Digital Library Initiative (CDLI) and the Database of Neo-Sumerian Texts (BDTNS), has it been possible for scholars to begin to organize the documents and to reconstruct the archives that must originally have existed at Puzrish-Dagan (as well as at other sites). Any individual tablet does not tell us much, but viewed in groups they are much more informative. One can trace the careers of individual officials, or examine the taxes paid by specific provinces in different years, or try to understand the principles that underlay the taxation system, or even look at the role of blind workers, or the responsibilities of messengers. Almost nothing this detailed has survived from any other ancient civilization.

The end of the Third Dynasty of Ur

Like all its precursors, the kingdom of the Third Dynasty of Ur came to an end, and the Mesopotamian cities over which it had ruled reverted to their more usual state of local control. For many of the people alive at the time, the change to their daily lives would have been minimal. Different rulers gave their names to the years, and taxes stayed close to home rather than being sent on to Ur, but rulers and taxes still existed, as did the need to plant and harvest, maintain irrigation canals, and to work on labor projects when called upon. Modern historians often see the end of the Third Dynasty of Ur as a significant turning point, and they have come up with many explanations for the end of the kingdom of the Third Dynasty of Ur: rebellions in some areas, invasions in others, expensive military campaigns against persistent enemies, pockets of poor harvests, climate change, possible displacement of the course of the Tigris, difficulties maintaining complex administrations, loss of taxes from the provinces. Any or all of these may have contributed to the end of the dynasty; the records are full of holes so it is hard to say. But for the average person living in Ur, or in another city that had paid its taxes to Ur in the past, the end of the dynasty might not have immediately seemed to be terribly important.

The Third Dynasty of Ur was followed by an era known as the Old Babylonian period, a time of large kingdoms primarily ruled by kings who spoke Amorite, a Semitic language that seems to have had western roots (Amorite means "western"). Although some important changes took place under the Amorite kings, they also adopted many of the institutions that had developed in the time of the kings of Ur.

The Ur kings had created a model of kingship that was emulated in later generations. Letters supposedly written by and to the kings of Ur were copied by generations of young scribes as part of their formal training. Like Ur-Namma and Shulgi, some subsequent kings aimed to be loved instead of feared (or loved as well as feared), perhaps concluding that loyalty was deeper if it was heartfelt rather than forced.

Chapter 6
The Old Assyrian colonies, 1950–1740 BCE

In the twentieth and nineteenth centuries BCE, Mesopotamia and Syria were not united under a single government. After the breakup of the empire created by the Third Dynasty of Ur, the new, smaller kingdoms vied for power, fighting with one another over borders and attempting to prevent vassals from changing allegiance. Kings forged alliances with one another against other kings, sent troops to one another's lands, and sometimes were able to seize control of foreign vassal kingdoms. This was also a time of extensive trade over surprisingly long distances.

Trade had always been a part of Mesopotamian life. Thousands of years before writing was invented, valuable stones like obsidian and lapis lazuli had reached Mesopotamia from Anatolia and Afghanistan. In the Early Dynastic period trade seems to have been mostly a royal concern; for example, the kings of Lagash mentioned trade with Dilmun (Bahrain). The king of Ebla had sent gifts to the king of Hamazi, hundreds of miles away. Sargon had boasted of ships from Meluhha (the Indus Valley) tying up at the quay of Akkad.

The best evidence for trade at the beginning of the second millennium BCE comes not from Mesopotamia or Syria but from Anatolia. More than sixty years of excavations at the ancient city of Kanesh (modern Kültepe, in central Turkey) have exposed more than

23,000 cuneiform tablets, mostly found in the houses. They attest to a close relationship between Kanesh and Assur in northern Mesopotamia, cities that were as far apart from one another as New York is from Chicago or as London is from Madrid: about 1,200 kilometers (about 750 miles). Assur was an heir to the cuneiform tradition. Its people were familiar with laws, long-distance diplomacy, cuneiform letters, and so on. Kanesh, though equally sophisticated in its architecture and art and boasting a powerful king and organized government, was relatively new to the cuneiform world.

The connection between the two cities had come about not because of warfare but because, in spite of the great distance that separated them (including mountains and deserts to be crossed) and their completely distinct cultures and languages, they needed one another. Kanesh had access to silver; Assur had access to tin and fine textiles. From around 1950 to 1740 BCE, Assyrian merchants traveled regularly to Kanesh, bringing goods to sell. Some of the Assyrians settled there in order to manage their businesses. They brought with them the cuneiform script, in which they recorded their transactions, and they also brought their expertise in creating treaties and contracts to consolidate and confirm their activities. Theirs were the houses in which the tens of thousands of cuneiform tablets were found. The era is referred to as the Old Assyrian period, to distinguish it from later eras in which Assyria (Assur) became a much great power, particularly the Neo-Assyrian empire, a thousand years later.

A trade treaty

One of the texts found in the ruins of a house was a copy of a treaty drawn up between the king of Kanesh and the Assyrian merchants. The tablet containing the treaty is, sadly, not well preserved and much of it is broken. Toward the end of the tablet the clauses are legible, but in the first half, not one line is complete. Still, one can see that the treaty begins with a listing of gods: "O Adad . . . gods of the land of Kanesh . . . Sin, Shamash." Although an Assyrian scribe wrote the tablet (the Assyrians were designated as "we" in the treaty, whereas the people of Kanesh were "you"), the gods they called on were from both lands, including, from Mesopotamia, Adad (the storm god), Sin (the moon god, equivalent to Sumerian Nanna), and Shamash (the sun god), along with the gods of Kanesh. This had been typical of Mesopotamian and Syrian treaties for centuries. Formal agreements required the involvement of the gods of both parties.

The first legible provisions of the treaty, after nine lines that are too broken to read, concern various kinds of cloth (there is unfortunately no way to know what the textile terms mean). These provisions were addressed to the king of Kanesh: "[If a] . . . textile . . . pleases your eye you shall not take it away by force. You shall not purchase it at a low price. From the *kutanum*-textiles—after you have taken the . . . tax, you can take [4?] *makuhum*-textiles (and) 2 *kutanum*-textiles."

The Assyrians were masters at finding cloth to sell in Anatolia. The textiles they brought from Mesopotamia were so prized by the Anatolians that the merchants were able to profit handsomely. The Assyrians bought fabric from the best workshops, most of which were in southern Mesopotamia. The merchants loaded the textiles onto donkeys (each donkey could carry about twenty-five of them), traveled the six-week-long journey to Anatolia, and sold them for two or three times what they had originally paid.

The Assyrians had names for the various types of fabric. The treaty mentions *kutanum*, *makuhum*, and *parakannum* textiles (and others), but we do not know what they looked like, only that some were more expensive than others. An Assyrian trader, though, would not only have recognized the weave, quality, and in some cases the patterns of each, but would have known which fetched the best prices. These were certainly much more than simple bolts of cloth. They must have been distinctive, like later Persian carpets, Navajo blankets, or Chinese silks. Although the people of Kanesh had their own weaving traditions and access to plenty of wool from their own herds of sheep, their local weaves seem to have been valued less than the foreign goods. Something the southern Mesopotamian artisans did, in their spinning, dying, or weaving of the wool, or in subsequent embroidering or sewing made the textiles both appealing and impossible to reproduce locally. Even the Assyrians could not match them. Although they sold some Assyrian textiles, the merchants worried a great deal when access to goods from southern Mesopotamia was disrupted.

The king of Kanesh, who lived in an impressive palace within the walls of his city, had his own taste in these fabrics. The traders paid him a tax, as specified later in the treaty: "For every 10 *parakannum*-textiles you will take 1 *parakannum*-textile as your . . . tax." In return he protected the traders, and the treaty made sure that he dealt fairly with them. They allowed the king the pick of their shipments, but he had to pay full price, and he could not simply appropriate any of the textiles.

It has been estimated that, in a period of around forty or fifty years, the Assyrian merchants brought as many as a hundred thousand textiles to Kanesh to sell—four thousand donkey-loads. As far as we know, every last one of the textiles has long since disintegrated. All that is left are the cuneiform tablets recording the Assyrian merchants' attention to the all-important acquisitions and sales.

The other major trade good that the Assyrians brought to Anatolia was tin. Here, too, the Assyrians served as middlemen. Tin originally came from somewhere in Iran or Afghanistan. As with the textiles, the Assyrians purchased tin, transported it, and sold it to the Anatolians. Although there is no reference to tin in the surviving section of the treaty, it might well have been mentioned in one of the broken sections. To the Assyrians' customers, tin was even more valuable than were the textiles, and therefore it created an even bigger profit. Tin was needed in the manufacture of bronze, for which the Anatolians had ample copper supplies in their region.

Unlike wool, tin was not to be found in Anatolia, so the locals had no choice but to purchase it. In a forty- or fifty-year period, more than twenty tons of tin traveled from Assur to Kanesh.

After the merchants who traveled from Assur to Anatolia had paid their taxes and visited the king to let him choose which goods he wanted to buy, they set about selling the rest of their wares in exchange for silver or gold. They even sold most of the donkeys that had transported the goods, keeping only a few to transport the silver home again. They did not, however, sell everything right there in Kanesh; some of the goods continued on, to be sold in other Anatolian cities, at an even higher price. It was a thoroughly successful and profitable arrangement, agreeable to both the Assyrians and the Anatolians.

The treaty shows, though, that sometimes things could go wrong. Assyrian merchants could even be murdered when in Kanesh. One clause reads: "If the blood of a citizen of Assur is shed in your city or in your land (and) a loss will occur, you shall pay the fixed amount for the blood-money to us and we will kill him (i.e., the murderer). You shall not give another person instead of him (the murderer) to us." The local authorities therefore owed the Assyrians more than simply the imposition of the death penalty on the murderer; a "fixed amount" of "blood-money" had been predetermined. The king of Kanesh ended up paying for the fact that the crime took place in his land.

Likewise the local king had to pay if textiles were stolen from the merchants in Kanesh: "If there is someone who lost his textiles in your city or country, you (the local king) shall look for (the textiles) and return them (to the owner). If you cannot find them (the losses), the owner of the losses will swear and you shall pay in full (for) the losses." One sees here that the man who suffered the loss had to swear an oath to the gods that he was telling the truth about it; as with the rest of the Mesopotamian judicial system, his willingness to swear to the gods that he was telling the truth was proof enough that he had indeed lost what he claimed. Then the king compensated him. This worked as a kind of insurance for the merchants and must have inspired the local king to help keep them and their wares safe.

Other clauses dealt with resolving debts between citizens of Assur and of Kanesh, with protecting the possessions of the Assyrian merchants, and with ensuring that they were not liable for labor service in Kanesh. All of these provisions were thoroughly practical and would have helped facilitate trade between the two states. The relationship between them had no military component; the treaty included no pledge of support in the case of rebellion or invasion, no concern with recognition of heirs to the throne, or any of the other usual clauses found in peace treaties. The Assyrians were welcome in Kanesh under the terms of the treaty not because their king had allied himself with the king of Kanesh but because the merchants provided goods and services that the Anatolians wanted.

Assyrian merchants and kings

Although they dealt directly with the king of Kanesh, the Assyrian merchants were not sponsored by their own king of Assur. They were entrepreneurial men who had forged and expanded their businesses largely without state support. For that matter, the king of Assur was not, in this era, a strong figure. He did not wield anything like the kind of power that the Third Dynasty kings of Ur or the Akkadian emperors had enjoyed. He did not even have the same clout as his contemporaries in southern Mesopotamia. The Assyrian king was constrained by a council of elders in the city; the king was at their head, but they made decisions, which he enforced. Each year one citizen of Assur, chosen originally by lot, was required to fill an office that oversaw the collection of taxes in the kingdom (in the south this was a kingly duty). In recognition of this official's efforts, his name was used from then on to refer to the year in which he served. So, whereas in much of the rest of Mesopotamia each year was named for a great deed accomplished by the king, in Assur each year bore the name of an official. The Mesopotamians did not yet number the years, so scribes created lists of the names of the years in order to keep track of them.

The Assyrian merchants' businesses were family ventures. There were at least ten powerful trading families based in Assur who did business in Kanesh and elsewhere in Anatolia. The men in a family business referred to one another as "father," "brother," or "son," and some of them, at least, do seem to have been family members. Others, though, used the same terms in order to reflect the hierarchy within the business, even if they were not related to the family. The "father" was the boss, the "brothers" were associates, and the "sons" were employees. This was a common Mesopotamian practice. Allied kings, for example, were described as "brothers," overlords were "fathers," and vassals were "sons" even when they had never even met one another.

The merchants lived in houses outside the city center of Kanesh. Although often referred to as an Assyrian "colony," it was not exactly that. The Assyrians lived among Anatolians in what was already an established town. Their houses were indistinguishable from those of their neighbors, as were their pottery and other household items. When the houses were excavated, only the merchants' cuneiform tablets and cylinder seals revealed them to be foreigners. They referred to their community as a *karum*, which normally means "harbor" in Akkadian. But there was no waterway at Kanesh. The *karum* was a trading quarter, part of the expansive circular lower city that extended around the central tell and that seems to have been more than three kilometers across.

Around 1836 BCE the trading quarter burned to the ground, an event that was devastating to the merchants. Probably some of their precious textiles were destroyed inside the burning houses. The inferno was helpful to modern archaeologists and historians, though, in that it baked and preserved the tablets right where they had last been consulted. Later the *karum* at Kanesh was rebuilt, and Assyrian merchants continued to live and trade there for a hundred years more, but they built over the mess of the burned houses rather than sorting through the ruins.

The activities of Assur-idi, merchant

About half of the documents found in the burned houses were letters. One such letter had been written by an elderly man named Assur-idi, who was the head of the family firm; he lived in Assur. He began his letter in the usual way, "Thus (says) Assur-idi: say to Assur-nada." Assur-nada was Assur-idi's adult son who had moved to Kanesh to serve as the main representative of the business there. Much of Assur-nada's time in Kanesh was taken up with selling the tin and textiles that his father sent him from Assur.

Although Assur-nada and his father were frequently in contact with one another about sales and prices (we know this because many of the family's letters have been found), the father's tone in this letter was impatient and even angry. He launched right into a complaint about business:

> Why did you write this to me: "You promised me that I could pay (the balance of) my accounts with your silver!" I did not promise you that, but you implored me, and I offered you 20 *kutanum*-textiles in the presence of Assur-kashid.
>
> Once our business is finished, send me quickly the silver belonging either to the proceeds from the textiles or to those from the donkeys, (for a total) of 10 minas. I will buy 2 talents of tin and I will send them to you. . . . You should not spend any of my silver.

Assur-idi was reminding his son that he had sent him textiles and donkeys, and that he needed the proceeds quickly: ten minas (pounds) of silver were required so that he could buy two talents (approximately 120 pounds) of tin, which, in turn, he would send back to Anatolia so that Assur-nada could sell them.

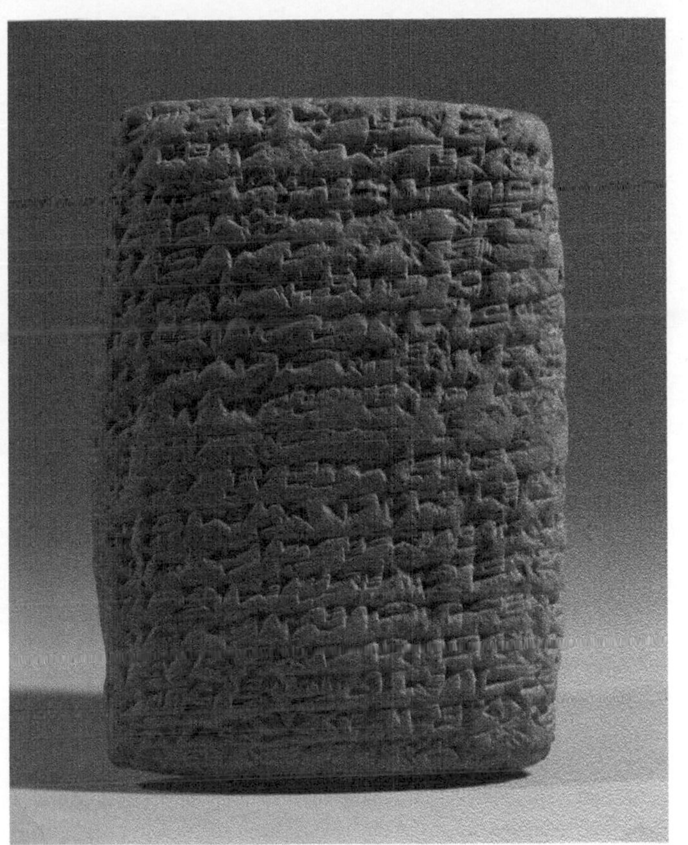

7. In this cuneiform letter found in Kanesh, the Assyrian merchant Assur-idi writes to his son Assur-nada about their trading operations transporting textiles to Anatolia.

The father and son kept separate accounts, as is clear from Assur-idi's insistence that Assur-nada not spend what he called "my silver," but they worked very closely together. The closeness is surprising, though, given that each of these letters would have taken about six weeks to arrive at its destination and the answer would not have come back for at least three months.

Assur-nada's other two brothers also worked in the family business. A younger brother did a great deal of the traveling, including sometimes returning to their father in Assur. Sadly, this brother died young of an illness. Assur-nada's letters show that, like his brother, he also traveled around to other cities in Anatolia, looking for places to sell his tin and textiles. On occasion he might even have returned to Assur (at least, his father pleaded for him to do so), but mostly he employed other traders to travel back home.

When the family patriarch, Assur-idi, wrote his letter to Assur-nada, he was not only angry about business. He also had a personal crisis on his hands. He continued:

> I raised your son, but he said: "You are not my father," whereupon he left; I also raised your daughters, but they said: "You are not our father." On the third day they left and departed for you and now I want to know what you have to tell me.

When Assur-nada had gone to live in Kanesh, he had left his son and daughters at home in Assur to be raised by their grandparents since their mother was dead. But now the children (who were presumably grown) had left for Anatolia as well, to be with their father. They had even said to their grandfather Assur-idi "You are not our father!" This was a particularly powerful statement in Mesopotamia, one with legal implications. A husband divorcing his wife had to speak the words "You are not my wife!" and a father renouncing his adopted son had to say "You are not my son!" Assur-nada's children were formally breaking their ties with their grandfather to rejoin their father and his new Anatolian wife in Kanesh. We know from other letters that as an adult, Assur-nada's son took up residence in a different city in Anatolia, working as a merchant, but that, like his uncle and so many others in the ancient world, he died young.

It is telling (and typical of the Assyrian merchants) that in the letter Assur-idi wrote about business matters first, mentioning the family crisis almost as an afterthought. His grandchildren renouncing him and leaving for Anatolia must have had a bigger impact on Assur-idi's life than the need for this particular payment of silver, but business came first.

Mesopotamian letters were rarely affectionate. In fact, they often sound curt. This might have been because they used no equivalents for "please" or "thank you" in regular conversation. But what sounds to us like rudeness would have seemed quite normal to Mesopotamian ears. Also, letters were not private. If either the sender or the recipient was illiterate (which was true of many Mesopotamians though not, usually, of the merchants), the letter would have been dictated to and read aloud by a scribe, who might well have been a stranger. This too argued against the expression of intimacies. Letters were written almost exclusively when important news or requests had to be communicated. No one would hire a messenger to take a letter more than twelve hundred kilometers simply to write about the weather.

Merchants were not only important in northern Mesopotamia and Anatolia; throughout the Near East their activities were integral to many aspects of society. For example, toward the end of the time of the Assyrian trading outpost at Kanesh, in the 1750s BCE, the Mesopotamian king Hammurabi put forward a set of laws for his extensive kingdom. Among them were twenty-eight laws (about 10 percent of the total) that governed the activities of merchants and traders. With their considerable wealth and their knowledge of foreign lands, these men had many responsibilities: they were expected to ransom soldiers who had been taken hostage (for which they could expect to be repaid); they served as bankers, lending silver at the hefty rate of 20 percent interest and grain at an astounding 33 percent interest to farmers, gardeners, and others who needed it; and of course they invested in trading ventures. One can give names and life stories to the merchants at Kanesh, but thousands of others like them helped drive the Mesopotamian economy throughout its history.

Chapter 7

The Old Babylonian period, 2004–1595 BCE

Around 1770 BCE a governor, Itur-Asdu, sent a letter to his "lord" King Zimri-Lim of the Syrian kingdom of Mari. Itur-Asdu told the king: ". . . with regard to what my lord wrote to the kings, saying, 'Come to the sacrifice in honor of Ishtar,' I gathered the kings to Sharmaneh." Zimri-Lim had apparently written a previous letter, probably to his vassals ("the kings"), asking them to attend a festival for Ishtar, just as the earlier kings of the Third Dynasty of Ur had gathered together envoys from surrounding lands for the religious festival in the city of Tummal. The kings accordingly had gathered in Sharmaneh, a city in one of the vassal provinces.

Itur-Asdu, for some reason, felt the need on this occasion to remind them of the wider political situation of Mesopotamia and Syria, beyond the boundaries of the kingdom of Mari:

> There is no king who is strong just by himself. Ten (to) fifteen kings are following Hammurabi the man of Babylon; so, too, Rim-Sin the man of Larsa; so, too, Ibal-pi-El the man of Eshnunna; so, too, Amut-pi-El the man of Qatna; (and) twenty kings are following Yarim-Lim the man of Yamhad.

Archaeological finds and other cuneiform documents confirm that he was right in his description. As he noted, at this time a number of kings of large states—Babylon, Larsa, Eshnunna, Qatna, Yamhad, and Mari—each served as overlord to a dozen or more vassal kings who governed from cities within their kingdoms. Two other kingdoms were not mentioned in the letter: Ekallatum (which now included Assur), a kingdom fast declining in prestige and power, and Elam, in what is now Iran, which many of the Mesopotamian and Syrian kings viewed as greater than any of them. Many of these kingdoms were led by Amorite dynasties, descendants of the Amorites who had been moving into Mesopotamia ever since the Third Dynasty of Ur. Although some of their names were in the Amorite language, they had assimilated thoroughly into Mesopotamian ways of life.

Around 1808 BCE, before Itur-Asdu's letter was written, a king in northern Mesopotamia had proved himself to be particularly successful in battle and in taking over lands from his neighbors. His name was Shamshi-Addu. He had been able to control not only the land of Ekallatum but also the land of Mari—resulting in a kingdom that dominated a fertile swath of land throughout most of what is now northern Iraq and eastern Syria. His lands had been so extensive that he had appointed two of his sons to help him rule. They served as viceroys in the traditional capitals—Ekallatum and Mari—while he ruled from a new capital city between the two.

By the time Itur-Asdu wrote his letter, however, Shamshi-Addu was dead. The son who had taken over from him had not been able to maintain control of the western part of his state—the kingdom of Mari—which was once again independent and now under the capable control of King Zimri-Lim. The king of Ekallatum had been demoted, in fact, to such an extent that he was considered no more than a "son" of Zimri-Lim. This might well be why his name did not appear in the list of kings with vassals in Itur-Asdu's letter.

The empire of Hammurabi of Babylon

Most of the kings listed—Rim-Sin, Ibal-pi-El, Amut-pi-El, and Yarim-Lim—though powerful figures in their own time, are probably unfamiliar to most modern readers. One of them, though, Hammurabi of Babylon, is as close to a household name as one finds in ancient Near Eastern history. No world history textbook would be complete without him. And yet in this letter, he is described as being just one of a number of kings of equal influence; indeed Yarim-Lim of Yamhad had more vassals than Hammurabi did.

The reason that Hammurabi's name lives on is because of events that took place after this letter was written. Hammurabi eventually conquered even more land than Shamshi-Addu, ruling most of what is now Iraq and part of Syria, from the Persian Gulf in the south all the way north to Mari, beyond the northwest border of modern Iraq. The former kingdoms of Larsa, Eshnunna, and Mari, along with their vassal kingdoms, were all subsumed into the kingdom of Babylon.

Hammurabi proudly named a whole series of years after his conquests. In year 30 he recalled the dramatic defeat of the huge and powerful kingdom of Elam:

> (Year 30): The year: Hammurabi, the king, the powerful one, beloved of (the god) Marduk, by the supreme power of the greatest gods overthrew the army of Elam which had mobilized (the lands of) Subartu, Gutium, Eshnunna and Malgium en masse from the border of Marhashi; also he made firm the foundations of Sumer and Akkad.

The conquests of the kingdoms of Larsa and Eshnunna were commemorated in years 31 and 32, then in the name of year 33, he proudly recounted that he was victorious over his former ally, the kingdom of Mari.

These year-names were supposed to be written out to identify the date on almost every contract and administrative text written during that year. But each one took up lines and lines of writing, so they were usually abbreviated. Year 30 became "the year:

Hammurabi, the king, the army of Elam," or just "the year: the army of Elam." Year 32 was "the year: the army of Eshnunna," and so on. By naming the years this way Hammurabi made sure that no one forgot his great accomplishments. Each time anyone referred to the date of an event—a birth or death, say, in the "year of the army of Eshnunna"—they had to recollect the king's victory. But Hammurabi did not claim that it was all his own doing. In the long versions of the year-names the gods were credited as well. He had the help of "the greatest gods," of "An and Enlil." He was the "beloved of Marduk"—the city god of Babylon—and "beloved of An and Enlil." And he did more than conquer. His year-names make it clear that he also strengthened his empire, making "firm the foundations of Sumer and Akkad," digging canals and providing water, and restoring the lands, thereby taking on the traditional kingly roles of both pious conqueror and generous provider.

By his thirty-fifth year on the throne, Hammurabi's empire was complete. In the remaining eight years of his reign he boasted, in his year-names, of building city-walls and ziggurats (including one for Ishtar) in several cities.

One achievement did not make it into a year-name, but it is the one for which Hammurabi is best known. Toward the end of his reign he had a large stone stela set up in Sippar, with a sculpted image of himself praying to the god Shamash at the top, and inscribed all over its surface with more than 275 laws. Just like Ur-Namma, he proclaimed that these laws were designed "in order that the mighty not wrong the weak, to provide just ways for the waif and the widow." Hammurabi claimed that he favored the underdogs, protecting them from people who had more power. But he also wanted to look good in the eyes of future generations of kings, and to be able to guide them, at a distance perhaps of many centuries: "May any king who will appear in the future, at any time, observe the pronouncements of justice that I inscribed upon my stela. . . . If that man has discernment, and

8. This diorite relief sculpture sits atop the stela containing Hammurabi's laws. The Babylonian king stands in prayer before the seated figure of Shamash, the god of justice.

is capable of providing just ways for his land, may he heed the pronouncements I have inscribed upon my stela." Writing once again fulfilled its role, so dear to Mesopotamian kings, of allowing the king's words to survive long after his death and to instruct future leaders.

The laws themselves were concerned less with violent crime than with issues such as property ownership, inheritance, agriculture, military service, marriage and divorce—issues that affected many people. The punishments specified sometimes fit the crime in an eye-for-an-eye manner, and the death penalty seems to have been more common than in Ur-Namma's time. On the other hand, heavy fines were often the penalty of choice. And, as always, contemporary court records make no mention of the laws, and the punishments and fines actually imposed were often more lenient than those Hammurabi had indicated.

Daily life

Writing was taking on several new roles at this time. The era from around 2004 to 1595 BCE, usually known as the Old Babylonian period, witnessed an explosion in the variety of documents produced. Just like the Assyrian merchants in Kanesh, many Mesopotamians kept, in their own homes, letters they had received and records of transactions they had been involved in. Whereas during the Third Dynasty of Ur most of the documents that have been found were produced by the great institutions (the temples and palaces), in the Old Babylonian period vast numbers of documents were private: loans, rental agreements, sales (of houses, fields, slaves), marriage contracts, and letters, for example. People recognized the value of a written document in creating a permanent record and, when necessary, could hire a scribe to create one for them. Literacy had also become more widespread, at least to the extent that more individuals could read, even if they were unable to produce cuneiform documents themselves.

Archives have been found even in quite modest houses, owned by men who were far from wealthy. For example, a few decades after Hammurabi's death, a man named Bakilum, living in the city of Terqa, just north of Mari at the border of the Babylonian empire, kept a record of two fields that he had bought. Although each region had its own idiosyncrasies with regard to the legal clauses, this document is similar in intent to contracts found all across Mesopotamia and Syria. It had seven main parts. Each part provides its own small revelation about some aspect of daily life in this era—agriculture, family, society, the gods, money, and the legal system.

First, the scribe was careful to define what was being sold:

> A field (measuring) 8 acres in the irrigation district of Zinatum, in the city of Terqa;
> upper long side: field of Yakun-Addu, son of Yasu-Addu;
> lower long side: field of Kinanu, priest of Dagan;
> upper short side: field of Kinanu, priest of Dagan;
> lower short side: field of the palace.

A second field followed. The scribe made clear exactly which fields were involved by noting their size and location and the names of the men who owned neighboring properties. Mesopotamian fields were long and narrow—hence the specification of the "long" and "short" sides. Canals coursed along the edges of the fields, flowing downhill from the river, the levees of which could be breached to fill them with water. Farmers had to be careful to make sure that their canals did not flood their neighbors' fields; courts would find a man liable if the water from his broken dike destroyed another man's crops. Bakilum's newly acquired fields would have been sown with wheat or barley, which were processed to produce bread and beer for his family. These were the basic staples of the ancient Near Eastern diet. They were supplemented with fish from the rivers, vegetables and fruits from gardens (date palms were especially valued for their sweet fruits), cheeses, and (on rare occasions) meat.

The second part of the contract named the buyer and the sellers:

> The fields belong to Aku and Mar-eshre, sons of Idin-Rim.
>
> From Aku and Mar-eshre, sons of Idin-Rim, owners of the fields, Bakilum, son of Sin-nadin-shumi, bought them for their complete price.

In this instance, as in most contracts, all the parties were men, each of them further identified by the name of his father. The contract is full of names: the neighbors, sellers and buyer, the governor, seventeen witnesses, and a scribe (and the king, though he was not there for the creation of the contract). Almost all of them were described as the "son of" someone else. The concept of surnames had not yet developed so this was how most men and women were distinguished from others with the same given name. The exceptions were men who served as "king," "governor," "priest of Dagan," and "scribe"; their important titles took precedence over the names of their fathers.

Third came the price: "He paid 1 mina, 10 shekels (about 0.58 kilograms) of silver," which came to five shekels per acre. It was a hefty sum, equivalent to almost six years of wages for a manual laborer (who earned about a shekel a month). Silver was, by this time, the standard currency in use throughout Mesopotamia and Syria, though coins were not invented for another thousand years. Instead, a scale was used to weigh the silver each time it changed hands. The silver that Bakilum paid for his fields might well have originated in Anatolia, brought south by the merchants from Assur.

The legal status of the fields was then given: "The fields, legally established, are not subject to claims or release." This was important to include because, once every decade or so, a king of this period would proclaim a *mesharum*, or redress, which attempted to restore the economy and society to some ideal state that was thought to have existed in the past. In order to do so, the king cancelled all private (but not commercial) debts, freed all people who had been enslaved because of their debts, and restored to its original owner land that had been sold under economic stress. The sellers and buyer in Bakilum's contract, though, agreed that the fields would not be subject to such a reversion, even if the king were to issue a release edict.

Fourth were the penalties threatened against anyone reneging on the contract: "A claimant who makes a claim—(since) he has sworn in the names of (the gods) Shamash, Dagan, Itur-Mer and Kashtiliashu the king—will pay 10 minas of silver to the palace, (and) hot asphalt will be poured on his head."

At this point the gods were involved, as they were in just about every aspect of Near Eastern life. The parties had sworn an oath to several gods—to the sun god Shamash as the god of justice, and to local gods Dagan and Itur-Mer—as well as to the local king. This oath was crucial; just as the gods watched over a treaty to make sure that both parties upheld their commitments, so too they watched over a contract that had been sworn in their names. But punishment, in this case, would not only have come from the gods if a man broke the contract. Such a man would also have been required to pay ten minas of silver as a fine to the palace. This was nine times the cost of the field, fifty years of a laborer's wages. Paying a fine like that could have destroyed a family's livelihood. And, as was true of all contracts drawn up in Terqa (though this was almost unknown in other regions), a man who violated the terms of the contract would have had hot asphalt poured or smeared on his head, no doubt causing severe burns. These clauses served as a serious deterrent against any seller suddenly "discovering" that he had not, after all, received the full price for his fields. A fraudulent claim was a criminal offense.

The fifth part of the contract was a list of seventeen witnesses, along with the name of the scribe who wrote the contract. The witnesses included individuals who owned adjoining fields, a brother of the buyer, and various other men who are known from other sources to have been members of families in the neighborhood of Terqa in which Bakilum lived. The witnesses to a contract were never an afterthought; the contract was not binding unless they were present when it was drawn up. The written document might be lost or broken, but the witnesses could always be called upon in court to say that, yes, they had seen the silver change hands and the oaths sworn. Bakilum really did have a right to the land he had bought.

In the witness list there was no reference to the social class or age of the witnesses, and few of their professions were mentioned. Exact age did not concern the Mesopotamians. They probably had little idea of how old they were or when their birthdays might have been. Burials show that people tended to die in middle age (if they survived the treacherous years of infancy and childhood), succumbing to disease, childbirth, injury, infection, or accident. For this reason, in the witness lists one rarely finds the name of the father of a party to the contract; adult siblings usually served as one another's support network, and brothers tended to be close. They even lived near one another. Sale contracts for houses often reveal that the immediate neighbors to a house were the owner's brothers or cousins. Sisters moved away when they married, but they too stayed in contact with their siblings, often sending letters and gifts. A sibling who failed to do so sometimes received an angry letter from a brother or sister; staying in touch and sending gifts was expected. Good fortune was to be shared.

Having children was important; couples who proved to be infertile sometimes brought in a second wife (this was rare, otherwise) or adopted a son. A son usually followed in the footsteps of his father, learning his profession. A man's sons could also serve as witnesses to a contract, and some of them listed in this role might have been quite young. They provided a sort of insurance, in case the contract was challenged decades later when most of the other witnesses were dead.

Social class was a curious phenomenon in the Old Babylonian period. On the one hand, the Mesopotamians cared a great deal about status. They were aware of where they stood in various hierarchies, just as the kings knew (and argued about) which of them was a "brother" to the major kings and which was a "son." They did not, however, almost ever mention the social class of a specific individual when writing about him (unless the individual was a slave), even though laws varied depending on one's status.

Free citizens were members of the independent, *awilum*, class. This is sometimes misunderstood to have constituted a small elite, but in fact any man who farmed his own land or who was not dependent on someone else was an *awilum*. (*Awilum* could also simply mean "man.") Below the free citizens were men who worked for others or who farmed state or temple property, the dependent, *mushkenum*, class. They were not serfs, since they were not tied to the land. But a *mushkenum* was often looked down upon by an *awilum*. Lower still was the *wardum*, or slave. Slaves were largely prisoners of war or the children of other slaves, but a free Mesopotamian could become a slave. If a man got into to debt and was unable to pay back the loan (a frequent occurrence, given the 33 percent interest rate), he could sell his family and even himself into slavery to his creditor. But in a few years he was freed, and his debt was considered paid. The classes were therefore fluid—they were far from being components of a rigid caste system. A man could, conceivably, move in his lifetime from being an *awilum* to a *mushkenum* to a *wardum* and back again.

No women were mentioned in Bakilum's contract, and that too was normal. Wives and daughters are usually invisible in private Old Babylonian documents. The drawing up of a contract was usually a male concern. On the other hand, women could and did represent themselves in court and serve as witnesses, on occasion. They could own property and pass it down to their children. They could hold jobs—particularly as innkeepers, weavers, and spinners—and high priestesses were still powerful individuals, as they had been since at least the Early Dynastic period. Some female religious functionaries, required to remain unmarried, directed their estates with acumen and became wealthy, independently of their fathers and brothers.

On the other hand, women were far from being the social or legal equals of men. Adultery, for example, was defined differently for men and women. A woman committed adultery if she had sexual relations with anyone other than her husband, whereas a married man was free to consort with concubines and prostitutes. He was only required to stay away from respectable women. A man could readily divorce his wife (though he owed her alimony), but, according to the laws, a woman could divorce her husband only if she could prove to the city council that he had been maligning her undeservedly.

After the witnesses to the contract came the date, month, and year on which it was drawn up: "Month of Kinunum, the twenty-second day. The year: Kashtiliashu set up justice." The Mesopotamians had a twelve-month year in which the lengths of the months were based on the cycle of the moon, but they realized that this left them several days short of a solar year. Every few years they added an extra month to make up the difference. Although they did not date letters, in most regions they were careful to date documents that they planned to keep for a long time and to consult later, and a contract fell firmly into that category.

Finally, the seventh part of the contract, written along the edges of the main text, gives the names of the five people whose cylinder seals were impressed on the tablet. The seals were of two neighbors to the purchased property, along with the governor, the scribe, and one of the witnesses. The seals had been rolled across margins of the tablet before the words were written on it and then names were written next to each seal.

The end of Hammurabi's empire

Hammurabi's empire faced many of the same difficulties as the empires that came before. It lasted for two hundred years, but the area ruled by its later kings was much reduced. The area to the south of the Babylonian heartland rebelled soon after Hammurabi's death, and his successors recorded fighting against various foes. Notable among these were the Kassites, a foreign military threat whose homeland is uncertain. But the enemy that ultimately conquered Babylonia was the land of Hatti, led by king Mursili I. The people of Hatti, the Hittites, lived in Anatolia, near the region where Assyrian merchants had traded their textiles and tin. The Hittite army arrived in Babylon around 1595 BCE, apparently with little warning, sacked the city, and returned home. The resulting power vacuum was filled, in the sixteenth century BCE, by kings of a Kassite dynasty who took over control of Babylonia.

Chapter 8
The Late Bronze Age, 1595–1155 BCE

In the mid-fifteenth century BCE, the Egyptian pharaoh Thutmose III led his troops on a rampage through Mittani (a powerful kingdom that had expanded throughout Syria and northern Mesopotamia), looting cities and capturing prisoners. But the Mittanian army proved to be a formidable opponent, stronger perhaps than Thutmose had anticipated for a land that must have seemed to him to be in a distant and unimportant region of the world. The shock of contact was probably mutual: Egypt had not ventured so far north in earlier times, and now the Syrians were the unhappy targets of a new, impressive, and immensely rich imperial army. Another power threatened Mittani as well—the expanding kingdom of Hatti to the north. Not that the kings of Mittani were passive victims of their muscular neighbors; they too had designs on nearby lands with valuable natural resources and access to the sea. Only Babylonia under its Kassite rulers seemed comfortable within its borders during the turbulent fifteenth century BCE.

The hostilities did not last, though. When neither Egypt nor Mittani gained an upper hand, the kings forged an alliance that was both pragmatic and beneficial to both sides. Peace spread like a contagion. First the kings of Egypt and Mittani, then of Babylonia and Hatti, then of smaller lands like Alashiya (Cyprus) and Kizzuwatna (Cilicia) bound themselves together through oaths and agreements, trading daughters, ambassadors, letters, and expensive gifts. These kings became "brothers" who supported one another and even sometimes professed to love one another, notwithstanding that they probably had never met. Much of this era from 1595 to 1155 BCE, known as the Late Bronze Age, was notable for the kings' extensive use of diplomacy, tempering the relationships between great powers.

Royal marriages and messengers

In the reign of Pharaoh Amenhotep III, messengers carried many letters to Egypt from Tushratta, the king of Mittani. Almost all of them began exactly the same way:

> Say to Nimmureya (Amenhotep III), Great King, king of Egypt, my brother, my son-in-law, whom I love and who loves me: Thus Tushratta, Great King, the king of Mittani, your brother, your father-in-law, and one who loves you.

This effusive greeting is the antithesis of the curses that brought treaties and royal inscriptions to their snarling conclusions. Tushratta wanted only the very best for Amenhotep III and for his fellow king's family, military, and family. He wrote:

> For me all goes well. For my brother and my son-in-law, may all go well. For your household, for your wives, for your sons, for your men, for your chariots, for your horses, for your country, and for whatever else belongs to you, may all go very well.

The greeting was, admittedly, formulaic but it would not have been included had the two kings not been firm allies.

The letter continued on to its main point, a marriage that had been arranged between the two royal houses.

> I (Tushratta) have given him my daughter to be the wife of my brother (Amenhotep III), whom I love. May (the gods) Shimige

> and Shaushka go before her. May they make her the image of my brother's desire. May my brother rejoice on that day.

The two kings were "brothers" not only because they were equal in power but also because they were relatives by marriage. A Mittanian princess, Tushratta's sister, was already married to the pharaoh and, with this letter, Tushratta was sending his daughter to Egypt as well, one of a steady stream of princesses from across the Near East and Mediterranean who traveled to Egypt, with crowds of attendants, to become royal wives.

No military threats, not even veiled ones, darkened this letter or any of the letters that passed between the kings. Even though the kings got angry with one another from time to time, their moods tended to result from perceived snubs or inadequate gifts, not from political crises. The routine retaliation when such an impasse occurred was to prevent an ambassador from speedily returning home or to hold back a promised gift. More often, though, the ambassadors traveled freely and regularly between the allied lands, and their diplomatic efforts could be deeply appreciated. Tushratta wrote about the Egyptian officials that

> Mane, my brother's messenger, and Hane, my brother's interpreter, I have exalted like gods. I have given them many presents and treated them very kindly, for their report was excellent. In everything about them, I have never seen men with such an appearance. May my gods and the gods of my brother protect them.

The highest ambassadors, like Mane and Hane in this letter, were men of great power, men who were authorized to represent their kings in high-level negotiations, even to approve the choice of the king's bride. Guards accompanied them, but traversing the hundreds of miles between Mittani and Egypt could still be dangerous; travelers definitely needed the gods on their side to ward off bandits and to send good weather.

Tushratta's blessing, "May my gods and the gods of my brother protect" the Egyptian envoys on their return journey, was generous. Typically for the time, he acknowledged the power of the foreign gods as well as his own to protect the Egyptian men when they traveled. The Mittanian princess, however, did not apparently need the help of Egyptian gods. According to this letter Shaushka (another name for Inanna/Ishtar), the principal goddess of Mittani, along with Shimige, god of the sun, would watch over the king's daughter as she made her way to Egypt.

At the end of almost every letter, the writer described a valuable gift that he was sending along. In this case Tushratta wrote:

> I herewith dispatch to my brother. . . . 1 *maninnu*-necklace of genuine lapis lazuli and gold as the greeting-gift of my brother. May it rest on the neck of my brother for 100,000 years.

A necklace was a relatively small greeting gift. Greeting gifts could sometimes be so extensive that they must have slowed down the messengers' travel—chariots and horses, furniture, raw materials, even people could be sent. Many greeting gifts were made of gold or silver and semiprecious stones, and must have represented the height of craftsmanship in the royal court from which they were sent. No specific objects found at an ancient site have been correlated to gifts mentioned in a letter, but artifacts do show that an international royal style developed at this time, a style that defies attempts to pin it to one region. Perhaps royal craftsmen were trained in multiple workshops in different places, taking ideas from each, or perhaps they were influenced by the many foreign objects that passed between the courts.

The necklace sent by Tushratta might not have been distinctively Mittanian in appearance. It might have incorporated some Babylonian, Hittite, or Aegean motifs and techniques. Even the materials from which it was made were not local. The lapis lazuli had come from the Hindu Kush Mountains, and the gold was making a return journey, having originated in Egypt. Mittanian jewelers worked their magic on the raw materials in such a way that the resulting necklace was worthy of the pharaoh. Tushratta hoped that it would be worn for "100,000 years"—because to him the alliance with Egypt seemed eternal, stretching ahead into future times no one could possibly imagine.

The Amarna letters

One striking fact is that all the letters sent between the great kings during this period were written in cuneiform on clay tablets, mostly in the Akkadian language. This is unsurprising for letters from Babylonia or Mittani, but it was also true of the letters sent by the Egyptian kings. For them, the script, the medium, and the language were all completely foreign. Egyptian scribes had to be trained in Mesopotamian scribal practices so that they could communicate their kings' words to their allies. The diplomatic conventions that the Egyptians were willing to follow were also alien. The whole system of foreign relations that had been created over the course of a millennium in Syria and Mesopotamia was adopted wholesale by the Egyptians and by the Hittites when they joined the international community.

The kings' letters caused quite a stir when they were first found in 1897—here were cuneiform documents not in Mesopotamia or Syria but in Egypt. Dozens of them were uncovered in Amarna, the site of the capital city of Egypt during the reign of King Akhenaten, and they are therefore known as the Amarna letters. Until their discovery, no one suspected that relations between the great powers had been so close during the Egyptian New Kingdom.

The alliances between the great kings did not, of course, prove to be eternal. They did, however, bring a remarkable level of peace and prosperity to the Near East and the Mediterranean for two centuries, an international age of cooperation. This is not to suggest that wars never took place. They did. Indeed, Mittani fell victim to the Hittites long before the end of the international age. But the kings of the great powers kept in diplomatic contact with one another and for the most part maintained peace, happy to enjoy the luxury goods that came their way and the building projects they could undertake with funds that might otherwise have gone to military campaigns.

Peace treaties

The peace was reinforced by formal treaties that had been negotiated between each pair of allies. Few of the treaties survive, unfortunately, though their existence is implied in the letters sent between the great kings. The kings often referred to treaty-based alliances as "friendly relations" between them and expressed the need to reaffirm these relations when a king died and his successor took over. So, for example, after a new pharaoh took the throne in Egypt, the Hittite king Suppiluliuma wrote to him of "the request your father made, saying 'Let us establish only the most friendly relations between us,'" and of his own desire for a continued alliance: "Just as your father and I were desirous of peace between us, so now too should you and I be friendly with one another." Most important to Suppiluliuma was that luxury gifts from Egypt keep coming: "Whatsoever your father said to me, I indeed did absolutely everything. And my own request, indeed, that I made to your father, he never refused; he gave me absolutely everything. . . . My brother, do not hold back anything that I asked of your father."

The best-preserved treaty from the international period was drawn up in 1260 BCE, a century and a half after the first treaties between the great powers, and it marked the end of a period of hostility between Egypt and Hatti. In it, King Ramesses II of Egypt made peace with King Hattusili III of Hatti. Very similar versions of the treaty have been found in Egypt and in Hatti. Earlier treaties between great powers were probably similar.

The goal of the treaty, in both versions, was "good brotherhood and good peace" to last forever, a relationship "which the Sun-god (of Egypt) and the Storm-god (of Hatti) established for Egypt with Hatti in accordance with their relationship from the beginning of time, so that for eternity he might not permit the making of war between them." More specifically each king agreed about the other that "He is my brother, and I am his brother. He is at peace with me, and I am at peace with him forever. And we will create our brotherhood and our peace, and they will be better than the former brotherhood and peace of Egypt with Hatti." One version even mentioned the specific earlier treaties, including the one with Suppiluliuma, and the continuity between those and the one drawn up now.

After these repeated pledges of brotherhood and peace, the document moved on to how this would work in practice. The kings first swore not to attack one another, then to defend one another if attacked by someone else, then to support one another's successors. A long section gave details on the treatment of fugitives. Most important was the next passage: the description of two thousand gods and goddesses of both lands who served as witnesses to the treaty. Without them the treaty was nothing but words on clay (or on silver, in the case of the official version). "A thousand of the male gods and of the female gods of them of the land of Hatti, together with a thousand of the male gods and of the female gods of them of the land of Egypt" could be counted on to enforce the treaty. Breaking the treaty was no small matter. A king who did so knew that the Hittite and Egyptian gods would "destroy his house, his land, and his servants." But if he kept to the treaty those same gods "shall cause that he be well, shall cause that he live, together with his houses and his (land) and his servants."

Each state was sovereign, and none of the great kings of the international period could claim to be more powerful than the others. If a king broke the terms of a treaty, no international body was standing by to step in with sanctions or reprimands.

But everyone agreed that the gods saw everything and could be counted on to enforce the oaths that had been sworn in their names.

A broken treaty and the plague

Suppiluliuma's life story had demonstrated the power of the gods (in the opinion of his son and presumably of the Hittite people more generally) to mete out punishments when a treaty was broken, specifically an earlier one between Hatti and Egypt. This is how his son Mursili II began the tale:

> . . . although the Hittites and the Egyptians had been put under oath by the Storm-god of Hatti, the Hittites came to repudiate (the agreement), and suddenly the Hittites transgressed the oath. My father (Suppiluliuma) sent infantry and chariotry, and they attacked the border region of Egyptian territory in the land of Amka.

King Mursili II was willing to acknowledge that his own father had broken a treaty. The punishment for this was imposed not just on the king but on the Hittite people as a whole, and it came directly from Egypt:

> When the (Egyptian) prisoners of war were carried off to Hatti, the prisoners of war introduced the plague into Hatti, and from that time people have been dying in Hatti.

What was the reason for this plague? Mursili suspected that the Hittite Storm-god brought it about in retribution for his father's impious act, so he asked an oracle:

> When I found the tablet mentioned earlier dealing with Egypt, I made an oracular inquiry of a god about it: "Has this matter discussed earlier been brought about by the Storm-god of Hatti because the Egyptians and the Hittites had been put under oath by the Storm-god of Hatti?"

9. This Syrian cylinder seal dates from the Late Bronze Age, when Syria was subject to the Hittites. The seal's impression shows a bull, with a male kilted figure on the bull's back, possibly an image of the storm god, and a stag.

Suppiluliuma had gone against the terms of his treaty with Egypt when he invaded Egyptian lands, so the gods were maintaining their side of the arrangement by bringing plague and death to the Hittites:

> It was ascertained (through an oracle) that the cause of the anger of the Storm-god of Hatti, my lord, was the fact that . . . the Hittites on their own suddenly transgressed the word (of the oath).

Even King Suppiluliuma himself had died as a result of the plague. The only remedy that Mursili could imagine was to pray to the Storm-god.

> I am now pleading my case concerning this to the Storm-god of Hatti, my lord. I kneel down to you and cry out: "Have mercy!" Listen to me, O Storm-god, my lord. Let the plague be removed from Hatti.

The gods were obviously impartial; the Hittite Storm-god did not side with his own people in this case but exacted his fury on them in such a devastating way that Mursili feared that the gods themselves would end up suffering. Hittite gods, like Mesopotamian ones, depended for their food, drink, and shelter on their people. But the plague did not discriminate—the men who made bread and beverages for the gods' sustenance were dying too. Mursili tried to reason with the gods:

> If you, the gods, my lords, do not send the plague away from Hatti, the bakers of offering bread and the libation bearers will die. And if they die off, the offering bread and the libation will be cut off for the gods, my lords.

Eventually the plague abated, but the story of its devastating impact, and of its cause, must have been told for generations. What we would see as an unlucky coincidence the Hittites saw as clear evidence of the power of the gods and the importance of adhering to the terms of a treaty. Even the oracles had confirmed that the broken oath caused the gods to bring the plague. What stronger proof could one ask for? Or what stronger incentive for being a good ally?

When Ramesses II and Hattusili III agreed to their treaty they cemented it with a royal marriage. A Hittite princess and her retinue traveled to Egypt and vast quantities of gifts were exchanged. This time, the brother kings kept their word—their messengers resumed regular journeys between the capitals at Thebes and Hattusa, and the lands stayed at peace. Tales about the plague no doubt helped keep them friendly. But even more compelling was their need to maintain a united front in the face of a growing threat in the east: Assyria, which was using military force to expand its domains. The Assyrian king believed that his successes qualified him to be considered a great king and an equal of the others, so he wrote to the king of Hatti as a "brother." The Hittite king was having none of it and wrote a very undiplomatic letter in response:

> So you've become a "Great King," have you? But why do you continue to speak about "brotherhood" . . .? For what reason should I call you

> my "brother"? . . . Were you and I born of the same mother? As my grandfather and father did not call the King of Assyria "brother," you should not keep writing to me about . . . "Great Kingship." It displeases me.

Hattusa, capital of the Hittite empire

The city from which the Hittite king wrote—his capital Hattusa—befitted a "Great King" in its fortifications and wealth. The unfortunate Assyrian messenger who eventually had to carry the blistering letter back to his king would have entered Hattusa through one of the three grand gates in the southern city wall. The one to the west was flanked by two stone lions, each seven feet high, the one to the east featured a statue of a king, and the central gate had a giant sphinx on each side. (Centuries later, the Neo-Assyrian kings adopted this same practice of placing huge stone sculptures of fantastic beasts on both sides of doorways and gateways.) The city was well protected, with double stone walls, atop precipitous cliffs in places, and regular towers positioned to rain arrows down on invaders. Hattusa was surprisingly remote, at the northern edge of the Hittite empire, so the walls protected the kings against hostile northern neighbors, not against Egyptians or Assyrians. Never did the forces from either land get even close.

Excavations at Hattusa (modern Boghazköy, 200 kilometers east of Ankara) began in 1906, and since then German archaeologists have unearthed dozens of monumental buildings (including many temples; it was a sacred place) along with streets and residential neighborhoods. At its height the city spread out over two square kilometers or about 500 acres. For a modern city this would be small but it was vast in ancient times, with perhaps forty thousand residents. Hattusa burned more than once, baking and shattering archives in many buildings. Archaeologists have recovered as many as twenty thousand fragments of cuneiform texts there.

The Hittites had learned the cuneiform script when they came in close contact with Syria and Mesopotamia, perhaps when the Hittite king Mursili I had attacked Babylon and brought an end to Hammurabi's empire. Their scribes sometimes wrote in Akkadian but also adapted the script to represent their own language of Hittite, which they called *nesumnili*, the language of Nesa (this was their name for Kanesh, the city that, long before, had been home to Assyrian merchants).

Hittite was an Indo-European language and is therefore related to English and most European languages, as well as to Persian and Sanskrit, and it was the earliest Indo-European tongue to be written down. But from earliest times the Anatolian region was home to many different peoples, speaking different languages, and these languages left their imprints on Hittite, which incorporated a number of foreign words. The cuneiform documents found at Hattusa attest to the multilingual population that thrived there. In addition to the many Hittite and Akkadian texts, others were written in Hurrian (the language of Mittani), Hattian (a local non-Indo-European tongue), and the neighboring Indo-European languages of Luwian and Palaic. Some inscriptions on stone were not written in cuneiform at all but in a pictographic script (confusingly called hieroglyphic, although it has no relationship to Egyptian hieroglyphs), used to render Luwian.

The end of the Late Bronze Age

Hattusa and the Hittite empire collapsed around 1200 BCE, but the exact circumstances that brought this about are unclear. The capital city was burned, so invaders seem to have played a major role, but their identity is uncertain. The hostile Kaska people who lived to the north might have been responsible, as might an enigmatic group who campaigned across the Mediterranean around this time—the "Sea Peoples" as they are generally known. The Hittite kingdom was already weakened when the invaders arrived, however. Around this time, a Hittite king wrote to a subordinate in Syria to plead for grain: "Why did it (a shipment of grain) remain with you even as much as one day? Don't you realize, my son, that there has been a famine in my lands?" Probably the entire region was suffering from a drought, and Hatti was more dependent on rainfall than were the river civilizations of Mesopotamia and Egypt. Peripheral regions of the Hittite Empire seem to already have gained their independence before the capital city was destroyed.

The Sea Peoples, a collection of refugees and fighters from the Aegean and other regions in the west, burned and looted cities along the eastern shores of the Mediterranean on their way to Egypt. One of their campaigns in northwestern Anatolia during this violent time might well have given rise to the legend of the Trojan War. The Egyptian king was able to repulse them, and many of them settled in the southern Levant. One of contingents of Sea Peoples, the Peleset, gave their name to the region where they settled: Palestine.

The chaos of these years had a domino effect. Whatever its causes—drought, famine, disease, refugee populations on the move—one result was the end of the international community of great kings. A weakened Babylonia was conquered by Elam, its eastern neighbor. Assyria contracted, losing its imperial possessions, though maintaining a continuous dynasty of kings. Hattusa was abandoned and its people dispersed. Even Egypt lost its unity, as a single king was unable to maintain control of the whole river valley. When a great power emerged again, almost three centuries later, it was not one that was willing to treat other kingdoms as equals—it was the first empire to dominate the entire Near East: Assyria.

Chapter 9
The Neo-Assyrian Empire, 972–612 BCE

For about 150 years after the end of the Late Bronze Age, from around 1155 to 972 BCE, small kingdoms came and went in Syria and Mesopotamia. To the west of the cuneiform lands, the kingdom of Israel was founded and flourished during this era, but other kingdoms left few records.

During this era of small kingdoms, Assyria, limited to a relatively small region around Assur, never forgot the greatness that it had formerly achieved. In the tenth century BCE its kings began to embark on campaigns to recapture lands that they perceived as their own, lands that their ancestors had ruled.

In the ninth century, King Assurnasirpal II was even more ambitious, venturing into areas that had never before been subject to Assyria. He used the wealth that flowed in as a result of his conquests to build a new capital city, Calhu. Its centerpiece was a sprawling palace that became a model for later kings to emulate. Its interior walls were covered with stone relief sculptures that towered over visitors, depicting the king at war, the king hunting lions, and the king in the company of gods, each panel accompanied by a cuneiform inscription extolling the magnificence and piety of Assurnasirpal. When the palace was complete, the king threw what might have been the biggest party that had ever been held. He claimed to have hosted 69,574 people from across his empire (and beyond) at a feast that lasted ten days. To feed them, he provided 27,000 cooked cattle, sheep, and lambs (to say nothing of the innumerable geese, ducks, gazelle, doves, and fish, along with vegetables and beer for all).

Assurnasirpal and his successors built an empire at least four times larger than any that had come before. Where, in the international age, there had been four or five major powers in regular diplomatic contact, now there was just one. The Assyrian kings' control over their empire was also more effective—and brutal—than had been true of earlier states. Their methods included the use of overwhelming military force to bludgeon and terrify their subjects and neighbors into submission, while making sure that well-protected roads allowed for the fast movement of troops and messages. At its height, the empire extended over all of what are now Iraq, Syria, and Lebanon, along with most of Egypt and parts of Iran, Jordan, Israel, Palestine, and Turkey. Almost all the cuneiform lands were under Assyrian rule.

The kings made little attempt to be loved or even liked by their subjects. They rejected the relatively friendly approach to empire espoused by their predecessors from the third and second millenniums BCE, such as Ur-Namma and Hammurabi. The Assyrian kings had gone back to the model set in place by Sargon of Akkad. They preferred to be feared.

In the centuries since, the Neo-Assyrian Empire has become almost synonymous with violence; its other achievements pale next to the memory of its military machine. Warfare dominated the public face of the Assyrian Empire. The triumphs of the army, and most notably of the king himself, were everywhere—not just in the reliefs that adorned the walls of the palaces but in inscriptions recording the highlights of each king's reign and in letters written between the king and his generals, officials, and diviners.

Military tactics and technology

Diviners were crucial because the king consulted them before making any major decision, military or otherwise: their ancient science revealed the will of the gods. To go against an omen or oracle would be as foolish as to swear a false oath. Omens might sound like superstition to a modern reader, but to the Assyrians they were regarded as reliable and verifiable. They had been recorded for thousands of years. When a remarkable event took place, such as an eclipse, a particular movement of a planet, or the occurrence of an unusual form in the liver of a sacrificial animal, diviners took note and then observed subsequent political events. These they took to be bound together. The astronomical sign or liver peculiarity had been a message from the gods that the political event was going to happen, and this was a predictive science. If the same sign was later observed, a comparable political event would follow. A deep knowledge of divination could help the king to maintain his power and expand his empire.

At one point in the seventh century BCE a diviner wrote a letter to the Assyrian king Assurbanipal about a number of signs that had been observed, among them the appearance of the planet Mars. The diviner in each case quoted a known omen relevant to the sign, and sometimes he added notes to show how this was relevant to the king's situation. He wrote that one old omen read: "If Mars appears in the month Ajaru, there will be hostilities. Affliction of the *umman-manda*." The diviner explained this to the king: "*Umman-manda* (means) the Cimmerians."

Mesopotamian astronomers had been observing the night sky for millennia; they knew when they could expect Mars to appear. In fact, they could even predict solar and lunar eclipses. But the predictability did not nullify the meaning of the omen. The Cimmerians could be expected to be hostile if the planet Mars was visible in the month of Ajaru.

The kings' relentless push to expand the boundaries of their empire (goaded on by assurances from the diviners that their aggression had the support of the gods) was rewarded by vast amounts of wealth that poured into the Assyrian heartland from booty and tribute. The army grew ever larger as recruits were brought in from conquered territories. Whole city populations were deported from one end of the empire to the other. Removed from their homelands, former rebels scrambled just to survive and to make a living. Rebel leaders were treated with an unprecedented brutality. In their royal inscriptions, the kings boasted of the horrific and gruesome ways in which they had tortured and killed their enemies. These kings were not "shepherds" of their populations, as earlier kings had described themselves. They did not mention protecting widows and orphans, as Hammurabi had done. They boasted instead of inspiring terror; in this they succeeded.

Conquest by Assyria, execution of the regional leaders, and deportation of the population was the fate of many kingdoms. One of them was a small western land known to the Assyrians as Bit-Omri. It barely registered in the minds of Assyrian kings, appearing almost without comment in lists of conquered territories. But the writers of the Bible called this land Israel, and they despised the Assyrians for how Israel was treated. Their writings, and their hostile view of the Assyrians, long outlived the empire itself.

Ever since the beginning of kingship in Early Dynastic times, rulers had portrayed themselves as chosen and protected by the gods. A king did not just order his troops into battle from the comfort of his palace; he led his forces in the field. The Assyrian kings continued this tradition and further exaggerated it. Each king depicted himself (in both relief sculptures in his palace and in royal inscriptions) as fighting on the front lines in every campaign, his chariot leading his soldiers into the fray. The kings are shown, alarmingly, unprotected by armor or helmets as they fought. This

10. A relief sculpture from the wall of King Assurnasirpal II's palace at Calhu shows the Assyrian king (*left*) aiming his bow to shoot an arrow at an enemy city. A battering ram breaks down the city wall (*right*), and Assyrian archers help with the attack from the top of a siege tower.

was the image they wanted to project—invincible and immune to the dangers that would kill any other man. But in reality no king would have subjected himself to this kind of risk. Although they were certainly present and out in the field during the wars, the kings probably watched from a safe distance. One letter to King Esarhaddon, Assurbanipal's father, belies the heroic image of the reliefs: "Of course, the king, my lord, should not go into the midst of battle! Just as other kings, your ancestors, have done, take position on a hill, and let your magnates do the fighting!" This would have made a much less impressive image for a palace wall, but it does help explain why so few Assyrian kings died on the battlefield.

The Assyrian army made use of the latest in technology, building on Mesopotamian military expertise accumulated over thousands of years of battles. The soldiers were expert bowmen—the bow was also the weapon of choice of the king. Bowmen could fight on foot, on horseback, or riding in chariots. For hand-to-hand combat a soldier might use a dagger, a short sword, or a mace, and spears were commonly employed against more distant targets. Long swords had not yet been invented; the iron forged by Assyrian blacksmiths was still too brittle. Helmets and shields (of varying sizes and shapes) protected the soldiers. Over time, chariots got higher, more maneuverable, and more impressive on the battlefield, drawn eventually by four horses and with a contingent of as many as four men in the cab (the driver, the bowman, and two shield bearers).

Relief sculptures also show Assyrian forces besieging cities: striking city walls with battering rams, scaling walls on ladders, firing arrows from siege towers, and digging tunnels under walls. A particularly effective strategy, if the city was next to a river, was to dam the river upstream, allowing the water to accumulate, then to breach the dam and let the water destroy the city wall. (This, ultimately, was how the Assyrian capital, Nineveh, was overcome in 612 BCE by the attacking Babylonians and Medes.) These technologies and strategies made the power of the Assyrian army prodigious. Lands within the empire might rebel, but like Israel they were always ultimately put down.

Assurbanipal the scholar

In a royal inscription, King Assurbanipal emphasized his physical prowess: "Ninurta (and) Nergal endowed my physique with manly vigor (and) unrivalled strength." But he was more than a warrior. Assurbanipal was also a scholar, and proud of it. Although he evidently studied for years with experts, the king credited the gods with his intellectual achievements. "Nabu, the scribe of the universe, made me a present of the precepts of his sagacity. I learnt the lore of the wise sage Adapa, the hidden secret of all scribal art."

Nabu was the god of wisdom and one of the main gods of the Assyrian kingdom, and the learning that Nabu had granted the king as "a present" certainly did set Assurbanipal apart from other rulers. Most kings had been illiterate throughout Mesopotamian history, relying on scribes, whereas Assurbanipal had been trained not just in reading and writing, but in many intellectual fields:

> I can recognize celestial and terrestrial omens (and) discuss (them) in the assembly of the scholars.
>
> I can deliberate upon (the series) "(If) the liver is a mirror (image) of heaven" with able experts in oil divination.
>
> I can solve complicated multiplications and divisions which do not have an (obvious) solution.
>
> I have studied elaborate compositions in obscure Sumerian (and) Akkadian which are difficult to get right.
>
> I have inspected cuneiform signs on stones from before the flood, which are cryptic, impenetrable (and) muddled up.

The four categories of knowledge that he mentions here are omen reading, divination, mathematics, and language and literature. These comprised much of the curriculum in Assyrian schools.

Mathematics was necessary so that scribes could accurately determine areas of fields, calculate rations and taxes, equitably divide inheritances, and so on. Hundreds of mathematical texts are known from the Neo-Assyrian period, including multiplication tables and geometric puzzles. Scholars had known how to calculate the hypotenuse of a right angle triangle a thousand years before the relevant theorem was named for Pythagoras, so it was already old knowledge by the Neo-Assyrian period. Assurbanipal seems to have been interested in theoretical mathematics, rather than in practical problems, as he worked on problems "which do not have an (obvious) solution."

One can sense Assurbanipal's pleasure at poring over "the cuneiform signs on stones from before the flood"—ancient documents in a form of script that was no longer in use—and perhaps discussing them with "the assembly of the scholars."

Scribes required sign lists in order to decipher antique texts, so Assurbanipal might well have felt the need for a particular list in order to make sense of these old inscriptions.

Expert cuneiform scholars, such as the ones with whom the king enjoyed arguing, often accumulated small collections of classic scholarly tablets for their own use. They copied them out by hand, adding a colophon at the end to record the source of the tablet and the scholar's own name, and to note that it was "for his reading." Assurbanipal seems to have had the same desire: he needed sign lists in order to decipher ancient texts, and series of omen texts in order to engage in debate with experts and to rule his kingdom. But he collected tablets on a much grander scale than anyone before him.

The library at Nineveh

When the Assyrian capital city of Nineveh was excavated by the British archaeologist Austin Henry Layard in the mid-nineteenth century, he discovered the remains of Assurbanipal's library in the impressive ruins of his palace. In Layard's report of the excavations, he wrote that his workmen had found rooms in the palace that "appear to have been a depository in the palace of Nineveh for such (cuneiform) documents. To the height of a foot or more from the floor they were entirely filled with them; some entire, but the greater part broken into many fragments." Modern archaeologists faced with such a treasure trove—cuneiform documents deposited a foot thick across a whole room—would meticulously record the findspot of every fragment. Unfortunately for us, this was not the practice in the nineteenth century. Layard's workmen put the tablets in boxes, without noting where they came from, and shipped them off to the British Museum. About twenty-six thousand tablets and fragments were excavated at Nineveh, most of them from four different buildings. We have no way of knowing exactly which of them were uncovered in the library room or what their findspots could have revealed about the order in which they were originally organized.

In building his library, Assurbanipal made a concerted effort to bring together documents from all over Mesopotamia. For example, he commanded the scribes in the Babylonian city of Borsippa to "Write out all the scribal learning in the property of (the god) Nabu and send it to me. Complete the instruction!" This might have seemed to be a daunting task, but the scribes responded enthusiastically: "Now, we shall not shirk the king's command. We shall strain and toil day and night to complete the instruction for our lord the king. We shall write on boards of sissoo-wood, we shall respond immediately." According to this letter, the copies that they made of the scholarly documents in the temple's possession were inscribed on wooden writing boards coated with wax rather than on clay tablets. If the documents were kept in this form in the library at Nineveh, they have long since disintegrated.

Assurbanipal's search for tablets to fill his library was methodical and painstaking. But his requests sometimes proved to be impossible to fulfill in the time he allowed. A scribe protested to the king in a letter written in 670 BCE: "Concerning the ritual about which the king said yesterday; 'Get it done by the 24th day'—we cannot make it; the tablets are too numerous, (god only knows) when they will be written." Some of the tablets in the library were copied in their place of origin and sent to Nineveh (for these, Assurbanipal paid handsomely), whereas some were appropriated from their owners, taken to Nineveh, and copied by scribes (imprisoned Babylonian scholars among them) before being returned. Almost all of them were masterpieces of orthography, every sign beautifully rendered. As Layard noted after the excavations: "The cuneiform characters on most of them were singularly sharp and well defined, but so minute in some instances as to be almost illegible without a magnifying glass." One wonders how the scribes could see clearly enough to write such tiny signs.

The type of scholarly knowledge that most intrigued Assurbanipal was the study of messages from the gods and ways to interpret them. These were the materials that were most valuable to him because, as he deeply believed, they could guide his decisions. "Send me tablets that are beneficial for my royal administration!" he wrote to a subordinate. Documents recording omens and oracles therefore formed the core of the library. Assurbanipal's love of learning had a practical side; the hundreds of omen texts that he collected could help him know when and how to fight. They are listed in the library's administrative records (some of which also survived), and they were found in huge numbers among the tablets excavated at Nineveh. Of the literary tablets (which probably came from the library) 739 contained lists of omens and how to interpret them, 636 were reports of omens observed and questions about them, but only 19 were epics or myths and another 19 were historical texts. (In spite of his claim to have mastered mathematics, Assurbanipal does not seem to have been quite as interested as he would have had us believe: only one mathematical text seems to have been found in the library.)

The epic of Gilgamesh

Among the tablets found by Layard in the library at Nineveh, the ones that created the greatest stir in the nineteenth century (once they were translated) were those that recorded an epic poem about a king who might have ruled almost two thousand years earlier: Gilgamesh. George Smith, a brilliant self-taught cuneiform scholar, was working at the British Museum, reading through the Nineveh tablets, when he recognized a story that was eerily similar to the biblical flood story. Here, in cuneiform, was the tale of a man who had been instructed by a god to build a boat in advance of a great flood and to fill it with animals. His boat floated as the storm raged and the world filled with water, and it survived the storm, eventually landing on a mountaintop. The man gave thanks to the gods for his survival.

The proper names were different, though, from those in the Bible. The survivor was Utnapishtim, not Noah, the god who warned him was Ea, not the biblical God, and the mountain where his boat ran aground was Nimush, not Ararat. Utnapishtim and his wife, unlike Noah, were given eternal life. But the parallels were remarkable and clearly not coincidental. The Mesopotamians and the Israelites had passed down what was essentially the same story over many generations. George Smith was so thrilled at his discovery that he impulsively "jumped up and rushed about the room in a great state of excitement, and, to the astonishment of those present, began to undress himself." The discovery caused a frenzy of media interest, and the British Museum still refers to the tablet as "the most famous cuneiform tablet from Mesopotamia."

The flood story was, however, a late addition to the Gilgamesh Epic, as it turned out. Mesopotamians had long believed in a great flood that had separated their prehistory into two parts. It was mentioned in the Sumerian King List, written more than a thousand years before Assurbanipal's reign, and a flood story very similar to that in the Gilgamesh Epic was first written down around 1700 BCE. A devastating flood in the region right at the beginning of the development of cities might well have caused such devastation that it passed into legend.

Gilgamesh, too, had been the subject of stories that had been told and written down for centuries. He probably was a historical king of the city of Uruk in the Early Dynastic period (though no direct evidence of him survives from that time), but by the Old Babylonian period he had become a superhero. Popular tales had him slaying fantastic monsters in the company of a champion named Enkidu, then vainly searching for immortality after Enkidu's death.

Late in the international period the Gilgamesh stories had been combined with the flood story. Assyrian scribes credited the resulting masterpiece to a writer named Sin-leqe-unninni. It was his version that was found (in four separate copies) in the library at Nineveh. He had placed Gilgamesh's quest for immortality as the central theme of the epic. Toward the end of the tale Gilgamesh manages to reach Utnapishtim, hoping to duplicate the hero's success at living forever. Utnapishtim tells Gilgamesh about the flood, but ultimately Gilgamesh reaches the conclusion that he is mortal and must die, and he reconciles himself to enjoying his earthly successes. The Gilgamesh epic was copied by scribes all over the Near East; copies have been found in Hatti, in Megiddo and Ugarit (near the Mediterranean coast), and in Emar (in Syria).

The end of the Assyrian Empire

The unprecedented success of the Assyrian military was ultimately undone not by a foreign power but by a series of civil wars between rival heirs to the throne. Assurbanipal fought and defeated his brother Shamash-shumu-ukin, who had been king of Babylon, after a long war, and civil wars continued in the reigns of Assurbanipal's sons. The decades of internal fighting weakened Assyria to such an extent that the Babylonians and Medes (from what is now Iran) were ultimately able to campaign far into Assyrian territory, destroying Nineveh in 612 BCE. If any of the subject peoples had dreams of independence, however, they were soon confronted with reality. The Babylonians and Medes divided the Assyrian Empire up between them—they were the new overlords.

Chapter 10
The Neo-Babylonian Empire, 612–539 BCE

The Neo-Babylonian kings, who took over control of Mesopotamia after conquering the Assyrians, did not boast of their violent victories over enemies. One looks in vain for references to impaling or flaying rebels in their inscriptions. No relief sculptures of chariots or troops graced the walls of their immense palaces. Instead, they were obsessed with building. By the end of the Assyrian Empire in 612 BCE, the cities of Babylonia were blighted by the ravages of war and neglect. The new local kings wanted to restore them to their former glory. Better yet, they wanted the cities to be even more glorious than before. New city walls, new temples, and new palaces went up, even bridges over the Euphrates.

Although the Neo-Babylonian kingdom was short-lived, surviving less than seventy-five years, its most prominent king, Nebuchadnezzar II, is one of the best-known figures of ancient history. This is due in part to his conquest of the land of Judah and the deportation of the Jewish people to Babylon, immortalized in the Bible. But he was also a builder, responsible for spectacular structures in Babylon, structures that still amazed the Greek historian Herodotus more than a century later. (It is unlikely that Herodotus visited Babylon, but he based his account on those of people who had.) Herodotus wrote of Babylon that "in magnificence there is no other city that approaches to it." And he had in mind, for comparison, the perfectly proportioned marble temples and elegant theaters of Greece. Later Greek and Roman authors credited Babylon with two of the seven wonders of the world: its city walls and Hanging Gardens (though, oddly, there is no contemporary evidence for the Hanging Gardens in Babylon; they might instead have been in Nineveh). The city was constructed of brick, so it has not weathered well, but in its time it was a revelation: its incomparably wide and strong walls enclosing what was then one of the largest cities on earth, its ziggurat touching the sky, its major thoroughfare flanked by walls of gleaming glazed bricks in vivid blue with relief sculptures of lions and fabulous beasts. The Babylonians thought of their city as being right in the center of the universe, home to the greatest of the gods, Marduk. Nebuchadnezzar's building program gave Babylon a grandeur appropriate to its political and religious importance.

Nebuchadnezzar not only beautified Babylon, he also oversaw the careful restoration of temples around the country. When he rebuilt the ziggurat in the nearby city of Borsippa he wrote, "I did not change its location and did not alter its foundations. In a propitious month, on an auspicious day, I (began to) repair the destroyed brickwork of its cella and its destroyed glazed brick covering (and to) set back up its ruined portions and I placed my own inscription in its repaired parts." This was typical of Neo-Babylonian kings: a respect for and desire to preserve past objects and buildings combined with a pride in their own architectural achievements.

Nabonidus

Nabonidus, the last of the Neo-Babylonian kings, followed in the steps of Nebuchadnezzar II, sponsoring building projects across his kingdom. In a long inscription he proudly described his reconstructions of three temples, including the temple of the god Shamash in Sippar. He began the inscription in the normal way, with his epithets and his claims of legitimacy:

> I, Nabonidus, the great king, the strong king, the king of the universe, the king of Babylon . . . for whom (the gods) Sin and Ningal in his mother's womb decreed a royal fate as his destiny, the son of Nabu-balassu-iqbi, the wise prince, the worshiper of the great gods.

Nabonidus did not refer to his father as a king, because he was not one. Two brief reigns ending in assassinations separated Nebuchadnezzar II from Nabonidus, and he was not in line for the throne. His surprising success at taking power was, he believed, ordained by Sin, the moon god, and foretold in a dream. Nabonidus did not feel that he owed his throne to Marduk, the city god of Babylon, but to Sin. Nevertheless, he was devoted to the care of all the gods, and the temple in Sippar dedicated to the sun god Shamash was in need of repair. The king wrote "For Shamash, the judge of heaven and the netherworld," he would repair the "Ebabbar, his temple which is in Sippar."

Shamash had always been the patron god of the city of Sippar, residing in his glorious temple called the Ebabbar (literally "the White House"). The temple provided a good proportion of the wealth of the city. Scholars estimate that the estates owned by the Ebabbar in the Neo-Babylonian period produced 1.2 million liters of barley and 1.8 million liters of dates each year. About one-sixth of this went to pay rations to workers, to feed animals, and to provide offerings to the god.

The Ebabbar had stayed in its traditional place although the city had moved away from it because continuity was important for temples. Each was on a sacred spot, the place where, at the beginning of time (to Mesopotamian minds) the gods had chosen to live, a place reaffirmed by omens and oracles. Any new temple had to be in exactly the right, traditional, and divinely ordained spot. The Ebabbar was where Shamash wanted to continue to live. But Nabonidus had some work to do; according to his inscription, the temple structure as it stood in his time was not worthy of the great sun god.

Before reconstruction could commence, the sun god himself (in the form of his cult statue) had to be moved, taken out of his home and given temporary quarters in another temple where he would continue to be fed, clothed, prayed to, and worshiped. Nabonidus described this process, and the subsequent search for the "foundation deposit"—the objects left in the foundations by the original king who built the temple: "While I led Shamash out of its midst (and) caused (him) to dwell in another sanctuary, I removed (the debris) of that temple, looked for its old foundation deposit, dug to a depth of eighteen cubits into the ground." Nabonidus set his archaeologists to work, digging down beneath the temple.

An earlier Neo-Babylonian king, Nabopolassar, noted that he used troops for excavating the foundations of a temple: "I levied the troops of (the gods) Enlil, Shamash and Marduk, had (them) wield the hoe, imposed (on them) the corvée basket (i.e., made them carry baskets of earth). . . . I removed its (the temple's) accumulated debris, surveyed and examined its old foundations, and laid its brickwork in the original locations." Nabonidus probably did the same, employing a large crew to dig with shovels, hoes, and baskets in search of the original location of the Ebabbar. They were lucky:

> . . . and (then) Shamash, the great lord, revealed to me (the original foundations) of Ebabbar, the temple (which is) his favorite dwelling, (by disclosing) the foundation deposit of Naram-Sin, son of Sargon, which no king among my predecessors had found.

Remarkably, Nabonidus's archaeologists found an original foundation inscription of the Ebabbar temple, one left by Naram-Sin, king of Akkad, about 1,700 years before. One senses Nabonidus's excitement when he stated that "no king among my predecessors had found" the ancient inscription before. Like the foundation inscription left by King Enannatum, who had ruled Lagash in the Early Dynastic period, this tablet would have recorded Naram-Sin's construction activities undertaken in devotion to the temple's god—Shamash in this case—and his blessings on any king who preserved the foundation inscription (along, perhaps, with curses on any king who moved it).

Later in the inscription Nabonidus mentioned Naram-Sin again: "The inscription in the name of Naram-Sin, son of Sargon, I found and did not alter. I anointed (it) with oil, made offerings, placed (it) with my own inscription and returned it to its (original) place." Nabonidus did what the earlier king must have instructed: he was respectful of the ancient object, anointing it with oil and reverently putting it right back where he found it. When the early kings had left these little time capsules in the foundations of their buildings, with their hopeful messages to some unknown readers far in the future, this was just what they had wanted: that kings, hundreds of years later, would acknowledge their great achievements (even mentioning the names of the long-dead kings in their own inscriptions) and treat with reverence the figurines and tablets that they had deposited.

Once the earlier foundations of the Ebabbar had been identified, new construction commenced. Only when the temple was complete was Shamash allowed to return, led back in a happy procession. Nabonidus wrote that "Ebabbar . . . I built anew and completed its work. I led Shamash, my lord, in procession and, in joy and gladness, I caused him to dwell in the midst of his favorite dwelling."

As always in Mesopotamia, much of the king's time and energy were directed toward assuring the happiness of the gods. Two thousand years after the first royal inscriptions were written, the kings still felt they owed their positions and the stability of their land to the gods, and in return they made sure that the gods had magnificent homes, their every desire and need addressed.

The New Year's festival

In Babylon the temple that crowned the city was dedicated to Marduk. Ever since the reign of Hammurabi, 1,200 years earlier, Marduk had been king of the gods in Babylonia. By the time

11. A clay cylinder records Nabonidus's reconstruction of three temples and his discovery of the foundation deposit left by Naram-Sin. The cylinder was excavated from the foundations of the temple to Shamash at Sippar.

of Nabonidus the temple complex was vast, encompassing two courtyards measuring a total of 90 m by 116 m (more than the size of two American football fields). The southern courtyard surrounded the Esagil, the rectangular temple of Marduk, and the adjoining northern courtyard surrounded a seven-story ziggurat. Marduk lived in the Esagil, his statue (according to Herodotus) "a sitting figure . . . all of gold. Before the figure stands a large golden table, and the throne whereon it sits, and the base on which the throne is placed, are likewise of gold. The Chaldaeans told me that all the gold together was eight hundred talents' weight" (22 tons).

Marduk, known respectfully as Bel or "lord," was the divine king of the land who, every year, was entreated to maintain the order of the universe over the course of a twelve-day New Year's celebration, called the Akitu festival, which took place in the spring. On the fifth day, the king and the god engaged in a curious interaction that was described in a later text. It began when the king arrived at the entrance to the sanctuary where the statue of Marduk was seated. A high priest called the *sheshgallu* approached him:

> When he (the king) reaches [the presence of the god Marduk/Bel], the *sheshgallu*-priest shall leave (the sanctuary) and take away the scepter, the circle, and the sword [from the king]. He shall bring them [before the god Bel] and place them [on] a chair.

The king was now bereft of his symbols of authority. His humiliation was far from over, however:

> He (the priest) shall leave (the sanctuary) and strike the king's cheek. . . . He shall accompany him (the king) into the presence of the god Bel. . . . .he shall drag (him by) the ears and make him bow down to the ground.

In this prone position, the king then proclaimed his piety and loyalty, to both his city and its great god:

> The king shall speak the following (only) once: "I did not sin, lord of the countries. I was not neglectful (of the requirements) of your godship. I did not destroy Babylon; I did not command its overthrow. I did not damage (?) the temple Esagil, I did not forget its rites. I did not rain blows on the cheek of a subordinate . . . I did not humiliate them. I watched out for Babylon; I did not smash its walls."

The priest responded with another scripted speech, after which "the king shall regain his composure. . . . The scepter, circle, and sword shall be restored to the king." But the priest had one more act to perform:

> He (the priest) shall strike the king's cheek. If, when he strikes the king's cheek, the tears flow, (it means that) the god Bel is friendly;

> if no tears appear, the god Bel is angry: the enemy will rise up and bring about his downfall.

This last section of the text reads something like the Assyrian omen documents collected by Assurbanipal. If a particular event took place, the conclusion was that Marduk was friendly, if its opposite occurred, then Marduk was angry. But the event that generated this message from the god was not the movement of a planet or the shape of a sheep's liver, it was the king shedding tears after being slapped in the face by a priest, and this after being stripped of his royal regalia, dragged by his ears, and forced to the ground.

It is hard to imagine any king consenting to such apparently humiliating treatment, but the Babylonians regarded this as a necessary part of the Akitu, their most sacred annual ritual. The significance of this ceremony has been debated extensively—perhaps it served as an annual re-coronation for the king; perhaps it symbolized the creation of chaos and restoration of order; perhaps the king ritually died and was reborn. Whatever the reason for it (and even the king and priest might have been unclear about this, given that it was already a very ancient ritual), it was necessary. It was also a private ceremony, witnessed only by the participants: the king and the priest.

In fact, most of the festival took place behind the closed doors of the temple. Hymns were sung, prayers pronounced, shrines purified, votive objects made and destroyed, and the entire text of the creation epic was read aloud to the god Marduk and his divine wife, Sarpanitum. The people of Babylon were not the audience for these ceremonies—they saw none of them. All the rituals and speeches were designed just to please the gods and to persuade them to maintain the divine order of their creation. When tears rolled down the king's cheek no crowd was cheering, but Marduk was there to see it.

The festival did have a public face, though. On the eighth day the god left his sanctuary. In a sacred place in the temple of the god Nabu, Marduk publicly pronounced the fates, his plans for the coming year (presumably communicating through a priest). Then he traveled in grand style along the wide Processional Way through Babylon. This was the most public part of the whole festival. The people of Babylon feasted and celebrated, and they lined the streets as the parade went by, hoping to catch a glimpse of their patron god. The king and Marduk rode at the head of the procession, followed by other gods and goddesses who had arrived from major cities of the empire for the occasion. All were dressed in luxurious garments and carried along in extravagantly decorated chariots, accompanied by musicians, singers, and dancers. Following the gods came the elites of Babylon—the priests, royal family members, and other influential citizens—along with prisoners of war and booty from military campaigns. In one place on this one day were displayed so much that made Babylonia great: its gods, its leaders, its wealth, evidence of its military success. The sight of it all must have awed—and reassured—the population.

The appearance of the king and the god together was referred to as the king "taking the hand of Marduk"—apparently the king literally held the hand of the statue. This phrase had come to signify the king's participation in the whole festival. Both the king and Marduk had to be in Babylon in order for the Akitu festival to take place. So, when the statue of Marduk had been captured, during the Neo-Assyrian Empire, the Akitu festival was postponed for years. The same was true if the king was not present: the Akitu had to be canceled. Most rulers who claimed to rule Babylonia (including earlier Neo-Assyrian kings and later Persian kings) made a point of being in Babylon for the New Year. "Taking the hand of Marduk" very visibly gave them the right to rule and assured the Babylonians that old traditions would be respected, even under a foreign regime. The phrase also had legal implications; through the performance of the ritual, the king and the god formally agreed to work together to protect and support the kingdom for the year.

The parade left the city through the Ishtar Gate, a tall building completely covered in gleaming blue tiles with glazed images of dragons and bulls in white, yellow, and blue. From there, the gods continued north by boat on the river until they reached Marduk's other home, the Akitu temple. For two days or more, the gods from all around the country conferred together at the Akitu temple, accepting offerings from the people. Then, on the eleventh day of the festival, another procession took place as the gods returned to the city. The festival ended with Marduk declaring the fates of the land for a second time, followed by an elaborate banquet, after which the other gods left Babylon.

King Nabonidus, the last Babylonian king, was not devoted to Marduk, however. He came from the Syrian city of Harran, which was a home to the moon god, Sin. Nabonidus was convinced that it was Sin, rather than Marduk, who had put him on the throne. This devotion to a god other than Marduk was highly unusual for a Babylonian king, and in some other ways as well Nabonidus acted strangely. According to many ancient sources, he left Babylon for ten years, putting his son Belshazzar in charge while he lived in the Arabian town of Tema—within his empire but far distant from the capital city. Did the Akitu festival take place in his absence? Later Persian sources say no, that it was canceled. The king's absence would have meant that no one could take the hand of Marduk; no one could help assure that cosmic order was maintained. One can imagine that the Babylonians would have felt less and less convinced of Nabonidus's legitimacy as king. A later chronicle recorded his absence every year:

> Ninth year. Nabonidus, the king, remained in the city of Tema.
>
> . . . In the month of Nisan, the king did not come to Babylon. Nabu did not come to Babylon. Marduk did not come out, and the Akitu festival was neglected.

Nabonidus eventually returned to the capital, when the forces of the expanding Persian Empire began to pose a serious threat to his kingdom. He gathered the gods of many cities (that is, their statues) into Babylon for protection, though the residents of those cities must have worried that they would be vulnerable without them.

The Persian conquest

The Persian conqueror Cyrus was able to use Nabonidus's quirks to his own advantage. In contrast to the long-absent Nabonidus, Cyrus claimed that he would be happy to take Marduk's hand if he ruled Babylon. Indeed, Marduk chose Cyrus for this very reason, so that order would return and the Akitu festival could proceed every year. Cyrus promised to return the gods to their proper cities and to allow deportees (the Jews among them) to return to their homes. According to Cyrus, the Babylonians welcomed him with open arms, happy to have a new king who venerated Marduk rather than Sin, and he claimed that he was able to take Babylonia without a fight. In reality, the Persians had to battle to take Babylon, and Cyrus was not especially devoted to Marduk. But the Persians acknowledged all gods, and the Babylonians were content to have the Akitu festival restored, even if it meant having a foreign king.

Babylon had accepted foreign rulers in Assyrian times, but those kings had usually sent a viceroy to live and rule in Babylon, and they shared a culture, language, and religion with the Babylonians. The Persian kings were different. Babylonia became a province in their vast empire, which stretched from the Indus Valley to the Aegean. Cyrus and his immediate successors turned up every year to perform the Akitu festival, but their capital was in Persia.

With Cyrus's victory, the era of Mesopotamian independence was over. Local culture changed only slowly after the Persian conquest, but in time cuneiform writing and the Akkadian language fell out of use, and the temples to the great Mesopotamian gods were abandoned. Someone must have melted down the gold statues of the gods, no longer fearing their wrath. The evidence for the splendid ancient Near Eastern culture eroded gradually away, the rivers changed their courses, and dirt and sand blew over the ancient cities. Thousands of years passed before modern excavations began and the world once more became aware of its first civilization.

of the gods, no longer fearing their wrath. The evidence of the splendid ancient Near Eastern culture faded gradually away, the rivers changed their courses, and dirt and sand blew over the ancient cities. Thousands of years passed before modern excavations began and the world once more became aware of its first civilization.

Chronology

(All dates are BCE and all dates prior to the Neo-Assyrian Empire are approximate)

Major eras and kings

The Uruk period 3500–2900 BCE

The Early Dynastic period 2900–2334 BCE

ca. 2500–2350	Lagash kings who fought with Umma (specific dates unknown)
	Eannatum of Lagash
	Enannatum of Lagash
	Enmetena of Lagash

The Akkadian Empire 2334–2193 BCE

2334–2279	Sargon of Akkad
2254–2218	Naram-Sin of Akkad

The Third Dynasty of Ur 2193–2004 BCE

c. 2150–2125	Gudea of Lagash
2112–2095	Ur-Namma of Ur
2094–2047	Shulgi of Ur

The Old Babylonian period 2004–1595 BCE

1950–1740	The Old Assyrian Colonies
1808–1776	Shamshi-Addu of Upper Mesopotamia
1792–1750	Hammurabi of Babylon
1822–1763	Rim-Sin of Larsa
1775–1762	Zimri-Lim of Mari
1620–1590	Mursili I of Hatti

The Late Bronze Age 1595–1155 BCE

1458–1425	Thutmose III of Egypt
1391–1353	Amenhotep III of Egypt
c. 1372–1326	Tushratta of Mittani
1353–1336	Akhenaten of Egypt
1344–1322	Suppiluliuma of Hatti
c. 1321–1295	Mursili II of Hatti
1279–1213	Ramesses II of Egypt
1267–1237	Hattusili III of Hatti

The Era of Small Kingdoms 1155–972 BCE

The Neo-Assyrian Empire 972–612 BCE

883–859	Assurnasirpal II of Assyria
680–669	Esarhaddon of Assyria
668–c. 630	Assurbanipal of Assyria

The Neo-Babylonian Empire 612–539 BCE

625–605	Nabopolassar of Babylon
604–562	Nebuchadnezzar II of Babylon
555–539	Nabonidus of Babylon
559–530	Cyrus of Persia

References

Chapter 2

Proto-cuneiform tablet: Hans Nissen, "The Archaic Texts from Uruk," *World Archaeology* 17 (1986): 317–34.

Chapter 3

Enannatum inscription: Donald P. Hansen, "Al-Hiba, 1968–1969, a Preliminary Report," *Artibus Asiae* 32/4 (1970): 243–58.

Inscriptions from Lagash: Jerrold S. Cooper, *Reconstructing History from Ancient Inscriptions: The Lagash-Umma Border Conflict* (Malibu, CA: Undena, 1983).

Glenn Magid, trans., "Enmetena" and "Urnanshe," in *The Ancient Near East*, ed. Mark W. Chavalas (Malden, MA: Blackwell, 2006), 11–14.

Accounts of the excavation of the Royal Tombs of Ur: Leonard Woolley, *Ur of the Chaldees: A Record of Seven Years of Excavation*, 2nd ed. (London: Benn, 1950), 45.

Leonard Woolley, *Ur: The First Phases* (New York: Penguin, 1946), 22.

Chapter 4

Sargon inscription: Benjamin Studevent-Hickman and Christopher Morgan, trans., "Creation of the Akkadian Empire," in Chavalas, *Ancient Near East*, 18.

Hymn to Inanna written by Enheduanna: Based on translation from the Electronic Text Corpus of Sumerian Literature, http://www-etcsl.orient.ox.ac.uk/section4/tr4072.htm.

Administrative text for gold jar: Alfonso Archi, "The Steward and His Jar," *Iraq* 61 (1999): 147–58.

Chapter 5

Laws of Ur-Namma (including the Prologue): Martha T. Roth, *Law Collections from Mesopotamia and Asia Minor*, 2nd ed. (Atlanta: Scholars Press, 1997), 15–17.

Calculation of the work on the ziggurat: Martin Sauvage, "La construction des ziggurats sous la troisième dynastie d'Ur," *Iraq* 60 (1998): 45–63.

Epilogue to the Laws of Lipit-Ishtar: Roth, *Law Collections*, 33.

Epilogue to the Laws of Hammurabi: Roth, *Law Collections*, 139.

Administrative text from Puzrish-Dagan: Tonia M. Sharlach, "Diplomacy and the Rituals of Politics at the Ur III Court," *Journal of Cuneiform Studies* 57 (2005): 17–29.

Chapter 6

Treaty between the cities of Assur and Kanesh: Cahit Günbatti, "Two Treaty Texts found at Kultepe," in *Assyria and Beyond: Studies Presented to Mogens Trolle Larsen*, ed. Jan Gerrit Dercksen (Leiden: NINO, 2004), 249–68.

Letter from Assur-idi: CCT3, 6b, text 254, Cécile Michel, *Correspondance des marchands de Kanish* (Paris: Les éditions du Cerf, 2001), 369.

Klaas R. Veenhof, "Old Assyrian and Ancient Anatolian Evidence for the Care of the Elderly," in *The Care of the Elderly in the Ancient Near East*, ed. Marten Stol and Sven P. Vleeming (Leiden: Brill, 1998), 122.

Chapter 7

Letter from Itur-Asdu to Zimri-Lim: Georges Dossin, "Les archives épistolaires du palais de Mari," *Syria: Revue d'art oriental et d'archéologie* 19 (1938): 117, trans. William L. Moran, *Ancient Near Eastern Texts Relating to the Old Testament*, 3rd ed. with supplement, ed. James B. Pritchard (Princeton, NJ: Princeton University Press, 1969), 628.

Year names of Hammurabi: Malcolm J. A. Horsnell, *The Year-Names of the First Dynasty of Babylon*, vol. 2, *The Year-Names Reconstructed and Critically Annotated in Light of their Exemplars* (Hamilton, ON: McMaster University Press, 1999), 139–47.

Epilogue to the Code of Hammurabi: Roth, *Law Collections*, 133–35.

Field sale contract: Text 1: Amanda H. Podany, *The Land of Hana: Kings, Chronology, and Scribal Tradition* (Bethesda, MD: CDL Press, 2002), 80.

Chapter 8

Letter from Tushratta to Amenhotep III: EA 21: William L. Moran, *The Amarna Letters* (Baltimore: Johns Hopkins University Press, 1992), 50.

Letter from Suppiluliuma to the Egyptian king: EA 41, Moran, *Amarna Letters*, 114.

Treaty between Egypt and Hatti: Text 15: Gary M. Beckman, *Hittite Diplomatic Texts*, 2nd ed. (Atlanta: Scholars Press, 1999), 97.

Egyptian version of treaty between Egypt and Hatti: "Egyptian Treaty" trans. John A. Wilson, in Pritchard, *Ancient Near Eastern Texts*, 200–201.

Prayers of Mursili II: Gary M. Beckman, trans., "Second Plague Prayer of Mursili II," in *The Context of Scripture*, 3 vols., ed. William W. Hallo and K. Lawson Younger Jr. (Leiden and Boston: Brill, 2003), 158; Beckman, trans., "Third Plague Prayer of Mursili II," in Hallo and Younger, *Context of Scripture* 2:159.

Letter from the Hittite king to the Assyrian king: KUB 23.102: Text 104: Harry A. Hoffner Jr., *Letters from the Hittite Kingdom*, Writings from the Ancient World 15 (Atlanta: Society of Biblical Literature, 2009), 323–24.

Letter from the Hittite king to a subordinate in Syria: Bo 2810: Text 120: Hoffner, *Letters from the Hittite Kingdom*, 363.

Chapter 9

Letter to Assurbanipal regarding omens: Text 110 = BM 98582: Simo Parpola, *Letters from Assyrian Scholars to the Kings Esarhaddon and Assurbanipal* (Winona Lake, IN: Eisenbrauns, 2007), 75.

Letter to Esarhaddon regarding staying out of the fighting: Text 77: Mikko Luukko and Greta Van Buylaere, *The Political Correspondence of Esarhaddon*, State Archives of Assyria 16 (Helsinki: Helsinki University Press, 2002), quoted in Andreas Fuchs, "Assyria at War: Strategy and Conduct," in *The Oxford Handbook of*

Cuneiform Culture, ed. Karen Radner and Eleanor Robson (New York: Oxford University Press, 2011), 382.

Royal inscription of Assurbanipal, king of Assyria: Asb. L i 11–18: Silvie Zamazalová, "The Education of Neo-Assyrian Princes," in Radner and Robson, *Oxford Handbook of Cuneiform Culture*, 315.

Report of excavation of the library at Nineveh and description of the tablets: Austin H. Layard, *Discoveries in the Ruins of Nineveh and Babylon* (London: John Murray, 1853), 345.

Letter from Assurbanipal regarding scribes in Borsippa: BM 45642, and letter from a scribe to Assurbanipal: SAA X 255 = AB: 18: Grant Frame and Andrew R. George, "The Royal Libraries of Nineveh: New Evidence for King Ashurbanipal's Tablet Collecting," *Iraq* 67 (2005): 265–84.

Letter from Assurbanipal requesting tablets: Andrew George, *The Epic of Gilgamesh: A New Translation* (London: Penguin, 1999), xxiv.

E. A. Wallis Budge describing George Smith: George, *Epic of Gilgamesh*, xxiii.

Image of the Flood Tablet from the Epic of Gilgamesh: http://www.britishmuseum.org/explore/highlights/highlight_objects/me/t/the_flood_tablet.aspx

Chapter 10

Description of Babylon: Herodotus 1.178.

Nabonidus's description of construction: Paul-Alain Beaulieu, trans., "The Sippar Cylinder of Nabonidus" in Hallo and Younger, *Context of Scripture*, 310–13.

Nabopolassar's description of construction: Paul-Alain Beaulieu, trans., "Nabopolassar's Restoration of the Imgur-Enlil, the Inner Defensive Wall of Babylon," in Hallo and Younger, *Context of Scripture*, 308.

Description of the Akitu Festival: E. Eberling, trans., "Temple Program for the New Year's Festivals at Babylon," in Pritchard, *Ancient Near Eastern Texts*, 334.

Chronicle recording Nabonidus's absence from Babylon: Bill T. Arnold, trans., "Chronicle 7" in Chavalas, *Ancient Near East*, 419.

Further reading

General works

Bienkowski, Piotr, and Alan Millard, eds. *Dictionary of the Ancient Near East*. Philadelphia: University of Pennsylvania Press, 2000.

Foster, Benjamin R., and Karen Pollinger Foster. *Civilizations of Ancient Iraq*. Princeton, NJ: Princeton University Press, 2009.

Kuhrt, Amélie. *The Ancient Near East c. 3000–330 BC*. 2 vols. London: Routledge, 1995.

Leick, Gwendolyn, ed. *The Babylonian World*. London: Routledge, 2009.

Leick, Gwendolyn. *Who's Who in the Ancient Near East*. London: Routledge, 1999.

Postgate, Nicholas. *Early Mesopotamia: Society and Economy at the Dawn of History*. London: Routledge, 1994.

Radner, Karen, and Eleanor Robson, eds. *The Oxford Handbook of Cuneiform Culture*. New York: Oxford University Press, 2011.

Roaf, Michael. *The Cultural Atlas of Mesopotamia and the Ancient Near East*. New York: Facts on File, 1990.

Roux, Georges. *Ancient Iraq*. Rev. ed. London: Penguin, 1993.

Sasson, Jack M., et al., eds. *Civilizations of the Ancient Near East*. New York: Charles Scribner's Sons, 1995.

Snell, Daniel C., ed. *A Companion to the Ancient Near East*. Malden, MA: Blackwell, 2007.

Van de Mieroop, Marc. *A History of the Ancient Near East*. Malden, MA: Blackwell, 2004.

Archaeology and Art

Akkermans, Peter M. M. G., and Glenn M. Schwartz. *The Archaeology of Syria: From Complex Hunter-Gatherers to Early Urban Societies (ca. 16,000–300 BC)*. Cambridge: Cambridge University Press, 2003.

Collon, Dominique. *First Impressions: Cylinder Seals in the Ancient Near East*. London: British Museum Publications, 1987.

Meyers, Eric M. *The Oxford Encyclopedia of Archaeology in the Near East*. New York: Oxford University Press, 1997.

Pollack, Susan. *Ancient Mesopotamia*. New York: Cambridge University Press, 1999.

Potts, Daniel T. *The Archaeology of Elam: Formation and Transformation of an Ancient Iranian State*. Cambridge: Cambridge University Press, 1999.

Historiography

Charpin, Dominique. *Reading and Writing in Babylon*. Trans. Jane Marie Todd. Cambridge, MA: Harvard University Press, 2011.

Chavalas, Mark W., ed. *Current Issues in the History of the Ancient Near East*. Claremont, CA: Regina Books, 2007.

Pedersen, Olof. *Archives and Libraries in the Ancient Near East 1500–300 B.C.* Baltimore: CDL Press, 1998.

Van de Mieroop, Marc. *Cuneiform Texts and the Writing of History*. New York: Routledge, 1999.

Literature and primary sources

Chavalas, Mark W., ed. *The Ancient Near East*. Malden, MA: Blackwell, 2006.

Cuneiform Digital Library Initiative (CDLI), http://cdli.ucla.edu/

Dalley, Stephanie. *Myths from Mesopotamia: Creation, the Flood, Gilgamesh, and Others*. New York: Oxford University Press, 2009.

Foster, Benjamin R. *Before the Muses: An Anthology of Akkadian Literature*. 2nd ed. Bethesda, MD: CDL Press, 1996.

George, Andrew. *The Epic of Gilgamesh: A New Translation*. London: Penguin, 1999.

Hallo, William W., and K. Lawson Younger Jr. *The Context of Scripture*. Boston: Brill, 2003.

Pritchard, James B., ed. *Ancient Near Eastern Texts Relating to the Old Testament*. 3rd ed. with supplement. Princeton, NJ: Princeton University Press, 1969.
Roth, Martha T. *Law Collections from Mesopotamia and Asia Minor*. 2nd ed. Atlanta: Scholars Press, 1997.

Aspects of Ancient Near Eastern Culture

Administration

Hudson, Michael, and Cornelia Wunsch, eds. *Creating Economic Order: Record-Keeping, Standardization, and the Development on Accounting in the Ancient Near East*. Bethesda, MD: CDL Press, 2004.
Nissen, Hans, Peter Damerow, and Robert Englund. *Archaic Bookkeeping: Writing and Techniques of Economic Administration in the Ancient Near East*. Chicago: University of Chicago Press, 1993.

Daily Life

Bottero, Jean. *The Oldest Cuisine in the World: Cooking in Mesopotamia*. Chicago: University of Chicago Press, 2004.
Nemet-Nejat, Karen Rhea. *Daily Life in Ancient Mesopotamia*. Westport, CT: Greenwood, 1998.
Snell, Daniel C. *Life in the Ancient Near East*. New Haven, CT: Yale University Press, 1997.

Diplomacy and Trade

Aruz, Joan, et al., eds. *Beyond Babylon: Art, Trade, and Diplomacy in the Second Millennium B.C.* New Haven, CT: Yale University Press, 2008.
Cohen, Raymond, and Raymond Westbrook, eds. *Amarna Diplomacy: The Beginnings of International Relations*. Baltimore: Johns Hopkins University Press, 2000.
Podany, Amanda H. *Brotherhood of Kings: How International Relations Shaped the Ancient Near East*. New York: Oxford University Press, 2010.

Divination and Astronomy

Rochberg, Francesca. *The Heavenly Writing: Divination, Horoscopy, and Astronomy in Mesopotamian Culture*. Cambridge: Cambridge University Press, 2007.

Law

Westbrook, Raymond. *A History of Ancient Near Eastern Law*. Leiden: Brill, 2003.

Religion

Black, Jeremy, and Anthony Green. *Gods, Demons and Symbols of Ancient Mesopotamia: An Illustrated Dictionary*. London: British Museum Press, 1992.

Bottéro, Jean. *Religion in Ancient Mesopotamia*. Chicago: University of Chicago Press, 2004.

Schneider, Tammi J. *An Introduction to Ancient Mesopotamian Religion*. Grand Rapids, MI: Eerdmans, 2011.

Specific Periods

Uruk, Early Dynastic, and Third Dynasty of Ur

Algaze, Guillermo. *Ancient Mesopotamia at the Dawn of Civilization: The Evolution of an Urban Landscape*. Chicago: University of Chicago Press, 2008.

Aruz, Joan, ed. *Art of the First Cities: The Third Millennium B.C. from the Mediterranean to the Indus*. New Haven, CT: Yale University Press, 2003.

Cooper, Jerrold S. *Reconstructing History from Ancient Inscriptions: The Lagash-Umma Border Conflict*. Malibu, CA: Undena, 1983.

Crawford, Harriet. *Sumer and the Sumerians*. Cambridge: Cambridge University Press, 1991.

Database of Neo-Sumerian Texts (BDTNS), http://bdts.filol.csic.es/

Michalowski, Piotr. *The Correspondence of the Kings of Ur: An Epistolary History of an Ancient Mesopotamian Kingdom*. Winona Lake, IN: Eisenbrauns, 2011.

Old Assyrian Colonies and Old Babylonian Period

Charpin, Dominique. *Hammurabi of Babylon*. London and New York: I. B. Tauris, 2012.

Charpin, Dominique. *Writing, Law, and Kingship in Old Babylonian Mesopotamia*. Chicago: University of Chicago Press, 2010.

Fleming, Daniel E. *Democracy's Ancient Ancestors: Mari and Early Collective Governance*. Cambridge: Cambridge University Press, 2004.

Heimpel, Wolfgang. *Letters to the King of Mari*. Winona Lake, IN: Eisenbrauns, 2003.

Van de Mieroop, Marc. *King Hammurabi of Babylon: A Biography.* Malden, MA: Blackwell, 2005.
Veenhof, Klaas R. *Aspects of Old Assyrian Trade and Its Terminology.* Leiden: Brill, 1972.

Late Bronze Age

Beckman, Gary M. *Hittite Diplomatic Texts.* 2nd ed. Atlanta: Scholars Press, 1999.
Bryce, Trevor. *The Kingdom of the Hittites.* Oxford: Clarendon Press, 1998.
Bryce, Trevor. *Life and Society in the Hittite World.* New York: Oxford University Press, 2002.
Feldman, Marian H. *Diplomacy by Design: Luxury Arts and an "International Style" in the Ancient Near East, 1400–1200 BCE.* Chicago: University of Chicago Press, 2005.
Hoffner, Harry A. Jr. *Letters from the Hittite Kingdom.* Writings from the Ancient World 15. Atlanta: Society of Biblical Literature, 2009.
Moran, William L. *The Amarna Letters.* Baltimore: Johns Hopkins University Press, 1992.
Van de Mieroop, Marc. *The Eastern Mediterranean in the Age of Ramesses II.* Malden, MA: Blackwell, 2007.

Neo-Assyrian and Neo-Babylonian Empires

Beaulieu, Paul-Alain. *The Reign of Nabonidus, King of Babylon 556–539 B.C.* New Haven, CT: Yale University Press, 1989.
Brinkman, John A., et al. *The Cambridge Ancient History.* Vol. 3, pt. 2, *The Assyrian and Babylonian Empires and Other States of the Near East, from the Eighth to the Sixth Centuries B.C.* Cambridge: Cambridge University Press, 1991.
Collins, Paul, et al. *Assyrian Palace Sculptures.* London: British Museum Press, 2009.
Curtis, John, et al. *The Cyrus Cylinder and Ancient Persia: A New Beginning for the Middle East.* London: British Museum Press, 2013.
Larsen, Mogens Trolle. *The Conquest of Assyria: Excavations in an Antique Land, 1840–1860.* London: Routledge, 1996.
Oates, Joan. *Babylon.* London: Thames and Hudson, 1986.

Index

Note: Page numbers in *italics* refer to illustrations.

A

Adad (god), 64–65
Adapa (legendary sage), 105
administration, 48, 53, 58–60, 61. *See also* officials
administrative texts
  Ur III administrative text, 59
  Uruk Period administrative text, 17–18
adultery, 56, 85. *See also* marriage
Aegean Sea, *12*, 90, *99*, 122
Afghanistan, 13, 37, 63, 66
afterlife, 38
agriculture, 12–13, 16, 53, 57, 61, 66, 80, 84
Akhenaten (king of Egypt), 91, 126
Akitu (New Year festival), 116–22
Akkad (land), *12*, *15*
  cuneiform script in, 7
  and kingdom of Kish, 36, 41
  origins of, 41
  in royal inscriptions, 45, 52, 57, 76, 77
  and Sargon, 41, 42
  and trade, 42
Akkad (or Agade, city), *14*
  and Sargon, 41, 42
  unknown location of, 50
Akkadian Empire, 40–50
  campaigns and conquests of, 40–43
  capital city of. *See* Akkad
  collapse of, 51
  and Ebla, 46–48
  innovations of, 48–50
  kings of, 125. *See also* Naram-Sin; Sargon
  priestess of, 43–46
Akkadian language, xvii, 33, 41, 43, 69, 91, 98, 106, 122
Alashiya (Cyprus), *12*, 87
Aleppo, 4
alliances, 37, 63, 87–89, 96–97
Amarna, *12*, 91
Amarna letters, 91–92
ambassadors, 47, 60, 87–90
Amenhotep III (Nimmureya, king of Egypt), 88, 126
Amorite kings, 62, 75
Amorite language, 62
Amut-pi-El (king of Qatna), 74–75
An (Anu, god), 45, 77
Anatolia (Turkey), *8*
  cuneiform script in, 7
  geography of, 13
  and Persian conquest, 15

Anatolia (Turkey) (*continued*)
and Sea Peoples, 99
and trade, 63–64, 65, 66–67
and Uruk-style artifacts, 24
animals. *See* donkeys; goats; sheep and goats
Anshan, *13*, 52
Anu. *See* An, 45
Arad-mu (official in Puzrish-Dagan), 59
Aramaic language, 15
archaeology, 2–6
ancient archaeologists, 115
modern archaeologists, 4–6, 31, 34, 37, 46, 60, 97, 107–8
art, statues and reliefs, 20, 37, 39, 48–49, 51, 53–54, 97, 100, 104, 113, 117
artisans, 35–37, 48, 66
Ashimbabbar (Nanna, god), 43, 44–45, 52. *See also* Sin
Assurbanipal (king of Assyria), 102, 105–9, 111, 126
Assur-idi's (Assyrian merchant) correspondence, 70–73
Assur-nada (Assyrian merchant), 70–73
Assurnasirpal II (king of Assyria), 100–101, *104*, 126
Assyria (Assur), *8*, *10*. *See also* Neo-Assyrian Empire; Old Assyrian colonies
cuneiform script in, 7
geography and climate of, 8–9
during Late Bronze Age, 96–97, 99
rivers of, 12–13
astronomy, 102–3
authorship, 44
awilum, 84

B

Babylon, *12*, *14*. *See also* Neo-Babylonian Empire; Old Babylonian period
governance of, during Old Babylonian period, 74–75
and Hammurabi's empire, 75–79, 98
and seven wonders of the world, 113
Babylonia, *10*. *See also* Neo-Babylonian Empire; Old Babylonian period
and Assyria, 105, 111, 112
cuneiform script in, 7
deities of, 114–15
in the Late Bronze Age, 87, 91, 99
and Nabonidus, 113–16
Bakilum, 80–81
Bakilum (resident of Terqa), 82–83
barley, 34, 53, 60, 80, 114
beer, 12, 17, 20–22, 25, 34–35, 80, 101
Bel (Marduk, god), 114, 115, 116–22
Belshazzar (prince of Babylon), 121
beveled-rim bowls, 20, 25
Bible, 2, 103, 109, 112
Bit-Omri (Israel), 103
bitumen, 13
boats, 9, 12, 13, 42, 60, 63, 121
borders, 36, 63, 76, 80, 104
Borsippa, *14*, 108, 113
breweries, 34–35
bronze, 25, 66
brotherhood. *See* alliances
burials, 3, 16, 83
royal, 37–38, 47

C

calendar, 55, 85
Calhu, 100
Canaan, 7, *8*
canals, 25, 61, 77, 80
carnelian, 13, 42
cemetery, discovery of, 37–39
ceramics. *See* pottery
chariots, 88, 90, 94, 103–5, 120
children, 29, 72, 83–84
chronology, 14
Cilicia (previously Kizzuwatna), 13

Cimmerians, 102
cities. *See* Akkad; Aleppo; Babylon; Calhu; Damascus; Ebla; Emar; Erbil; Eshnunna; Girsu; Habuba Kabira; Hamazi; Hattusa; Kanesh; Kish; Larsa; Mari; Nineveh; Nippur; Puzrish-Dagan; Qatna; Tema; Terqa; Ugarit; Umma; Ur; Uruk
cities, earliest, 16–26
- and deities, 20–21
- Uruk, 17–20
- and Uruk period, 23–26
- writing and documents from, 16–17, 21–23

city-states, 30
classes, social, 83–84
clay, 3, 17
climate, 2, 12–13, 99
colonies
- Old Assyrian colonies, 69–73
- Uruk colonies, 24–26

columns, 19
contracts, 3, 14, 55, 64, 76, 79–85
- Old Babylonian field sale contract, 80–85

copper, 13, 24, 31, 37, 42, 48, 52, 54, 66
council of elders, 68, 85
cradle of civilization, 1
craftsmen and craftsmanship, 48–49, 90–91
Creation Epic, 119
creation of humans, 28
cult statues, 20, 115, 120, 122
Cuneiform Digital Library Initiative (CDLI), 61
cuneiform lands, 6–7, 12–13, 101
cuneiform script, 6–7, 12, 32, 47, 64, 91, 98
- and Akkadian Empire, 47
- culture associated with, 15
- deciphering of, 2
- description of, 6
- in Early Dynastic period, 32–34
- and Hittite empire, 97–98
- obsolescence of, 122–23
- and Old Assyrian colonies, 64
- online archives, 61
- and Persian Empire, 14, 122
- proto-cuneiform, 17, *18*, 21–23, 26
- sequence of signs, 23
- writing names in, 22–23

currency, 81
curses, on inscriptions, 35, 57, 88, 116
cylinder seals, 21, 23–24, 26, 48, 69, 85, 95, 117
- of Akkadian Empire, 48
- of Late Bronze Age, *95*
- of Old Assyrian colonies, 69
- of Old Babylonian period, 85
- of Uruk period, 23, 26

Cyrus (king of Persia), 122, 126

D

Dagan (god), 82
Damascus, 1
Database of Neo-Sumerian Texts (BDTNS), 61
death, 83
death penalty, 56, 79
debts and debt release, 68, 81–82, 83–84
deities. *See* gods and godesses
deportation, 103, 112, 122
Dilmun (Bahrain), *9*, 23, 42, 51, 63
diplomacy, 42, 46–47, 59–60, 64, 87–92, 101. *See also* alliances
- in Akkadian Empire, 42, 46
- Amarna letters, 91–92
- ambassadors, 89–90
- and gift giving, 36, 46–47, 63, 89–91, 92, 96
- in Late Bronze Age, 88–92, 96–97
- in Old Assyrian colonies, 64
- royal marriages in, 88–89
- in Third Dynasty of Ur, 60

disease, 16, 83, 94–96, 99
divination, 102–3, 106, 114
divorce, 79, 85
Diyala River, *15*
documents, Akkadian period hymn of Enheduanna, 44–46
donkeys, 65–67, 70
Drehem (previously Puzrish-Dagan), *11*, 60

E

Ea (god), 110
Eanna temple, 18–19
Eannatum (king of Lagash), 35, 37, 125
Early Dynastic period, 27–39
  conflict in, 35–37
  cuneiform script of, 32–34
  kings and kingship in, 27–29, 33–34, 125
  and Lagash, 30–32, 35–37
  and royal tombs of Ur, 37–39
  temple and palace estates of, 34–35
  and Umma, 35–37
Ebabbar, 116
Ebabbar temple, 114
Ebla, *8*, 46–48, 63
Eblaite language, 47, 48
economy. *See also* trade
  private economy, 26, 42, 79
  and proto-cuneiform, 19–20, 21–23
  temples' role in, 22
  in the Uruk period, 17, 24
  women's work in, 24
Egypt, *8*
  writing system in, 7
Egypt, in late Bronze Age, 87–96, 99
  foreign relations in, 88–91, 92–93
  and Hatti, 94–96
  and international community, 99
  kings of, 87
  peace in, 87
Ekallatum, *10*, 75
Elam, *11*
  cuneiform script in, 7
  geography of, 13
  governance of, 75
  Hammurabi's conquest of, 76
  and international relations, 7
  in Late Bronze Age, 99
  and Persian conquest, 10–11
  and trade, 13
Emar, *8*, 111
Enannatum (king of Lagash), *30*, 31–32, 33, 34, 115
En-dingirmu (official in Puzrish-Dagan), 59
Enheduanna (priestess of Ur), 43–46
Enlil (god)
  divine kingship of, 28, 45
  and Lagash's borders, 36
  in offerings, 59
  in royal inscriptions, 40, 45, 52, 77, 115
Enmetena (king of Lagash), *36*, 37, 125
Era of Small Kingdoms, 126
Erbil, 4
Esagil temple, 117
Esarhaddon (king of Assyria), 104, 126
Eshnunna, *11*, 74–75, 76
estates, temple and palace, 22, 34–35, 42, 43, 84, 114
Euphrates River, *8*, *10*, 12
excavation, 4–6, 46, 63, 97, 107–8, 123. *See also* archaeology
experimentation, spirit of, 48–50

F

families, 69, 72, 81–84, 88. *See also* children
farming. *See* agriculture
festivals, religious, 59, 74, 116–21
fields, 12, 25, 34, 36, 39, 79–82, 106
fines, 56, 79, 82

flint, 25
floods, 12, 44, 80, 106, 109–11
food, 20, 22, 25, 37, 80, 100–101
  food for the gods, 28–29, 34–35, 96
foundation deposits, 31, 115
fugitives, 93

G

geography, Mesopotamia, 12–13
gifts
  in Akkadian Empire, 46–47
  at burial sites, 38
  as diplomatic gestures, 36, 46–47, 63, 89–91, 92, 96
  in Early Dynastic period, 31, 36, 38
  in Old Assyrian colonies, 63
  in Old Babylonian period, 83
  royal, in Late Bronze Age, 89–91, 92, 96
  royal gifts, 88–90, 92, 96
  between siblings, 83
  in temple construction, 31
Gilgamesh, epic of, 109–11
Girsu, *11*, 34, 36
goats. *See* sheep and goats
gods and goddesses, 16, 17–18, 20–21, 28–36, 39, 43–46, 51–52, 56–57, 59, 64–65, 67, 77–78, 82, 89–90, 93–96, 100, 102–3, 105, 109–10, 114–16, 118–23
  Adad, 64–65
  Adapa, 105
  and Akitu festival, 120
  An/Anu, 45
  and Assurbanipal, 105
  city gods, 30
  Dagan, 80–82
  Ea, 110
  in Early Dynastic period, 27, 30
  Enlil, 28, 36, 40, 45, 52, 59, 77, 115
  foreign gods, 89–90
  of Hammurabi's empire, 77
  hymns to, 44–45
  Inanna/Ishtar, 17–18, 20–22, 24, 31–34, 41, 43–46, 54, 57, 74, 77, 90, 121
  Ishtaran, 36
  Itur-Mer, 82
  and kings, 27–29, 52, 116
  kings presented as, 48, 57
  and legal system, 56
  Marduk, 76–77, 113–22
  Nabu, 105, 108, 114, 120–21
  Nanna/Sin/Ashimbabbar, 43, 45, 52, 59, 65, 114, 121–22
  of Neo-Assyrian Empire, 103, 105
  of Neo-Babylonian Empire, 116–22
  Nergal, 105
  Ningirsu, 30–31
  Ninsun, 52
  Ninurta, 105
  and oaths, 94–96
  offerings to, 21, 34, 44, 59, 114
  of Old Assyrian colonies, 64–65
  and origins of humanity, 28
  of Persian Empire, 122–23
  relationship of humanity with, 28–29
  Sarpanitum, 119
  Shamash, 64–65, 77–78, 82, 111, 113–17
  shared belief in, 30
  Shaushka, 89–90
  Shimige, 88, 90
  Shulutula, 31–32
  Storm-god of Hatti, 93–95
  and "taking the hand of Marduk," 120, 121, 122
  and trade, 64–65
  and treaties, 64–65, 93, 94–96
  in the Uruk period, 23
  and written communication, 33
  and ziggurat construction, 52–53
gold, 13–14, 16, 24, 37–38, 47, 67, 90–91, 117
graves, 37–39
Greece and Greeks, 2, *12*, 113
Gudea (king of Lagash), 51, 125

H

Habuba Kabira, 25
Habur River, *14*
Hamazi, *8*, 47, 63
Hammurabi (king of Babylon)
  dates of, 10, 125
  empire of, 75–79, 98
  laws of, 57, 73, *78*
  leadership style of, 101
  reign of, 14
Hane (Egyptian interpreter), 89
Hanging Gardens of Babylon, 113
Harran, *8*, 121
Harshi (ambassador from Elam), 59–60
Hatti, *8*, 87, 92–93, 94–96. *See also* Hittites and Hittite empire
Hattusa, *8*, 97–98, 99
Hattusili III (king of Hatti), 92, 96, 126
herding and herders, 16, 24
Herodotus, 112–13, 117
hieroglyphic script, 98
Hindu Kush Mountains, *13*, 90
Hittites and Hittite empire
  and Assyrian king, 96–97
  and Babylonian conquest, 86
  capital city of, 97–98
  collapse of, 98–99
  and cultural conventions, 7, 12
  and foreign relations, 91
  and Mittani, 92
hymns to the gods, 28, 44–46, 119

I

Ibal-pi-El (king of Eshnunna), 75
Ibgal temple, 31–32
Inanna (Ishtar, goddess)
  and Enannatum, 34
  festival for, 74
  and Hammurabi's laws, 57
  hymns to, 44–45
  and proto-cuneiform tablet, 17, 18
  and Sargon, 41, 43, 44–46
  statue of, 20
  temples of, 20–21, 24, 31–32, 34, 41
  and Uruk, 17, 20–21
  ziggurat construction for, 77
Indus Valley, 13
international style, 90
Iran, 13, 14, 24
  source of tin, 66
Iraq, 5, 7
Ishtar, 43, 45, 57, 74, 77. *See also* Inanna (Ishtar)
Ishtaran, 36
Ishtar Gate, 121
Israel, *8*, 100, 103, 110
Itur-Asdu (Old Babylonian period governor), 74–75
Itur-Mer (god), 82

J

jewelry, 24, 37, 90–91
Jewish people, 112, 122
Judah, 112
judges, 55–56
justice, 52, 55–57

K

Kanesh, *8*, 63–64, 66–68, *71*
karum, 69–70
Kashtiliashu (king in Terqa), 82, 85
Kaska people, 98
Kassite dynasty, 86, 87
kingdoms, vassal, 63, 74–76
King of Kish, 36–37, 40, 42
kings and kingship, 27–29, 41–42, 68–69, 125–26. *See also specific kings, including* Sargon
  of Assur in Old Assyrian period, 68–70
  on the battlefield, 103–4
  communication among, 33, 35–36, 91–92, 96–97
  deification of, 48–49, 57

and deities, 27–29, 34, 43–45, 52, 57, 90, 93–96, 103–5, 107–8, 114, 116
in Early Dynastic period, 27–29, *33–34*
and economy, 81
hereditary kingship, 27–29
literacy levels of, 105–6
of Neo-Assyrian Empire, 103–4
and royal tombs of Ur, 37–39
sculptures of, 48–49
and subjects, 62
of Ur, 57, 62
Kish, *11*, 23, 36, 41
Kizzuwatna (later Cilicia), *8*, 13, 87

L

laborers, 20, 25–26, 34, 53, 114
Lagash, *11*, 30–32
in Early Dynastic period, 30–32
in Gudea's reign, 51
palace estates of, 34
trade in, 63
and Umma, 35–37
land ownership, 42, 79, 80–82
lapis lazuli, 13, 42, 46, 63, 90
Larsa, *11*, 74–75, 76
Late Bronze Age, 87–99
Amarna letters of, 91–92
diplomacy in, 88–92
end of, 98–99
kings of, 126
peace in, 87–88, 91–92
plague in, 94–96
royal marriages in, 88–89
treaties in, 92–96
laws and legal system, 1–2, 51–52, 55–57, 79
Laws of Hammurabi, 57, 73, *78*
of Old Assyrian colonies, 73
of Third Dynasty of Ur, 51–52, 55–58
Layard, Austin Henry, 107, 108, 109
leaders, Uruk period, 20
letters, 35–36, 64, 70–73, *71*, 79, 87, 88–91
Amarna letters, 91–92
earliest letters, 35–36
in Early Dynastic period, 35–36
of Ebla, 46–47
between kings, 35–36, 62, 74–76, 88–90, *96–97*
Late Bronze Age Hittite royal letter, *96–97*
Late Bronze Age letter from Mittani, 88–91
of Neo-Assyrian Empire, 102, 104, 108
Neo-Assyrian letter about omens, 102
of Old Assyrian colonies, 70–73
Old Assyrian merchant's letter, 70–73
Old Babylonian letter to Zimri-Lim, 74–75
of Old Babylonian period, 74–76, 79–85
of Third Dynasty of Ur, 62
Levant, *8*, 99
lexical lists, 22, 48
Limestone Temple in Eanna precinct, 19
literacy, 33, 73, 79, 105–6
loans, 73, 79, 84
looting, 5
Luwian language, 98

M

Magan (Oman), *9*, 42, 51
Mane (Egyptian ambassador), 89
manpower, 25–26
Marduk (Bel, god), 114, 115, 116–22
Mari, *10*, *12*
and Akkadian Empire, 46, 48
and Old Babylonian period, 75, 76
and Sargon, 46, 48

marriage, 84–85
  diplomatic royal marriages, 47, 87–89, 96
  marriage contracts, 79
  royal marriages, 88–89
mass production, 24
mathematics, 1, 106, 109
me, 29
Medes, 105, 111
Mediterranean, *12*, *14*
  and cuneiform lands, 9
  geography of, 9
  peace in region, 91
  and royal marriages, 89
  and Sargon, 40, 41
  and Sea Peoples, 98, 99
Megiddo, *8*, 111
Meluhha (Indus Valley), *9*, 42
merchants, 58, 64–73
Mesalim (king of Kish), 36
mesharum, 81–82
Mesopotamia, *12*, *14–15*. *See also specific empires and eras*
  archaeological evidence of, 2–6
  astronomers of, 102–3
  climate of, 12–13
  and cuneiform lands, 6–7, 12
  and epic flood story, 110
  and international relations, 7, 91
  legal system of, 1–2
  and mathematics, 1
  and Persian conquest, 15
messengers, 26, 35–36, 61, 88–90, 96
metallurgy, 24
metal ores, 25
metals, 24, 25. *See also* bronze; copper; gold; silver; tin
Middle Chronology, 10
military, 42, 87, 96, 101, 103
military technology, 104–5
Mittani, *8*
  diplomatic gestures of, 88–91
  Hittite conquest of, 91–92
  peace in, 87
  Thutmose's attacks on, 87
months, 55, 60, 85
mountains, 13
mud. *See* clay
murder, 67
Mursili I (king of Hatti), 98, 125
Mursili II (king of Hatti), 94–96, 126
mushkenum, 84
musical instruments, 37
musicians, 120

N

Nabonidus (king of Babylon), *117*, 121–22, 126
Nabopolassar (king of Babylon), 115, 126
Nabu (god), 105, 108, 114, 120–21
names, 22
Nanna (Ashimbabbar, god), 43, 44–45, 52. *See also* Sin
Naram-Sin (king of Akkad), 48, 49, 57, 115–16, 125
natural resources, 13
Nebuchadnezzar II (king of Babylon), 112–13, 114, 126
Neo-Assyrian Empire, 100–111
  and Assurbanipal, 105–7
  capital city of, 100
  collapse of, 111, 112
  and Gilgamesh epic, 109–11
  kings of, 126
  and library at Nineveh, 107–9
  military machine of, 101, 102–5
  rise of, 99
Neo-Babylonian Empire, 112–23
  kings of, 113–16, 126
  and New Year's festival, 116–22
  Persian conquest of, 122–23
Nergal (god), 105
nesumnili, 98
New Year's Festival (Akitu), 116–22
Nimmureya (Amenhotep III, king of Egypt), 88, 126
Nineveh, *8*, *10*, 105, 107–9, 111, 113
Ningal (god), 114

Ningirsu (god), 30, 31
Ninsun (goddess), 52
Ninurta (god), 105
Nippur, *11*, 28, 40
numerical systems, 21
nutrition, 80. *See also* food

O

oaths, 56, 67–68, 82, 87, 94–96
obsidian, 13, 63
offerings to gods, 21, 34, 44, 59, 114
officials, 41, 59, 61, 81, 89
Old Assyrian colonies, 63–73
  and Assur-idi's correspondence, 70–73
  dates of, 125
  and deities, 64–65
  merchants and kings of, 68–70
  and trade, 63–68
Old Babylonian period, 74–86
  daily life in, 79–85
  end of, 85–86
  and Hammurabi's empire, 75–79
  kings of, 125. *See also* Hammurabi
  rise of, 62
omens, 102, 106, 109, 114, 119
oracles, 94–95, 102, 109, 114
order vs. chaos, 27, 29, 53, 117–19
origins of civilizations, 5

P

Pakistan, 14
palace estates. *See* estates, temple and palace
Palaic language, 98
Palestine, 99
past, Mesopotamian view of, 40
peace, 87–88, 91–94
Peleset, 99
Persia, 7, *9*
Persian Empire, 10–11, 121–23
Persian Gulf, *9*, *10*, *11*, 13
place names, 22–23
plagues, 94–96. *See also* disease
plains, Mesopotamian, 9
pottery, 23–25, 69
pottery wheel, 24
prayers, Late Bronze Age Plague Prayer, 94–96
priestesses, 37, 43–45, 84
priests, 20, 26, 34, 37, 80, 118–20
prisons, 56
private documents, 79
Processional Way, 120
property ownership, 79, 80–82, 84
Proto-cuneiform, 17, 20, 21–22
Puzrish-Dagan (later Drehem), *11*, 58–61

Q

Qatna, 74–75

R

rainfall, 12–13, 16
Ramesses II (king of Egypt), 92, 96, 126
rape, 56
rations, 19, 25, 42, 53, 114
rebellions, 31, 41, 51, 61, 68
reeds, 60
refugee populations, 99
religion, 17, 27–29, 43, 122. *See also* afterlife; divination; festivals, religious; gods and godesses; omens; oracles
resources, natural, 2–3, 13–14
Rim-Sin (king of Larsa), 75, 125
rivers, *8–9*, *10–11*, 12–13, 16, 25, 80, 105, 123
roads, 58, 101
Rome and Romans, 2
royal inscriptions, 31–32, 40–41, 44, 57, 88, 103, 105–7, 113–17
  Akkadian period royal inscription of Sargon, 40–41

royal inscriptions (*continued*)
Early Dynastic royal inscription of Enannatum, 31–32
Neo-Assyrian royal inscription, 105–7
Neo-Babylonian royal inscription, 113–17

S

sales, 66, 70, 79–80
salt, 9
Samsi-Addu, 75, 125
Sargon (king of Akkad)
and Anatolian plateau, 7
campaigns and conquests of, 40–43, 47
dates of, 125
and Inanna (Ishtar), 41, 43, 44–46
innovations of, 48
leadership of, 41–43, 101
military of, 42
and trade, 42, 51, 63
Sarpanitum (goddess), 119
scribes, 27, 32, 40, 53, 59, 62, 69, 73, 79, 91, 108, 110–11
sculptures. *See* art, statues and reliefs
Sea Peoples, 98–99
Semitic languages, 33, 41, 47, 62
seven wonders of the world, 113
Shamash (god), 64–65, 77–78, 82, 111, 113–15, 116–17
Shamash-shumu-ukin (king of Babylonia), 111
Shamshi-Addu (king of upper Mesopotamia), 75, 125
Sharmaneh, 74
Shaushka (goddess), 89, 90
sheep and goats, 7, 13, 16, 18, 21–22, 24, 59, 66, 101
shells, 9, 16, 38
sheshgallu priest, 118–19
Shimige (god), 88–89, 90
Shulgad (ambassador from Zidahri), 59
Shulgi (king of Ur), 55, 56, 57–58, 62, 125
Shulutula (god), 31–32
siblings, 83
silver, 9, 24, 37, 46, 47, 56, 64, 67, 70–71, 73, 81, 90
Sin (god), 65, 114, 121, 122. *See also* Nanna/Sin/Ashimbabbar
Sin-leqe-unninni (author of Gilgamesh epic), 110–11
Sippar, *10*, 77, 114
slaves, 56, 82, 84
Smith, George, 109–10
social stratification, 20, 83–84
standardizations, 52, 55
statues. *See* art, statues and reliefs, 20, 117
stelas, 48, *49*, 57, 77, *78*, 79
Storm-god of Hatti, 93–95
stratigraphy, 4
Sumer, 7, 8, *12–15*, 33, 36, 41, 46
culture of, 36
cuneiform script in, 7
and king of Kish, 36
in royal inscriptions, 52, 57, 76–77
Sumerian language, 32–33, 47, 48
Sumerian King List, 27–28, 110
Sumerian language, xvii, 28, 29, 32–33, 43, 47–48, 61, 106
Suppiluliuma (king of Hatti), 92, 93, 94–95, 126
Syria, *8*
climate of, 13
cuneiform script in, 7
cylinder seals of, 23
and Egypt, 87
geography of, 12–13
and international relations, 7, 91
looting in, 5
and Persian conquest, 11
rivers of, 12–13
and Uruk-style artifacts, 24

T

"Tablet of Destinies," 29
Taurus Mountains, 9, *12*
taxation, 55, 58–62, 66–67
  and Old Assyrian colonies, 68–70
  in Third Dynasty of Ur, 58–61
Tell Hariri (Mari), 46
Tell Mardikh (Ebla), 46
tells, 3–6
  growth of, 3–4
Tema, *8*
temples, 22
  construction of, 19, 52–53
  of Inanna in Lagash (Ibgal), 31–32
  of Inanna in Uruk (Eanna), 17–19
  of Marduk in Babylon (Esagil), 117
  of Nanna in Ur (Ekishnugal), 43
  of Shamash in Sippar (Ebabbar), 114
  temple estates. *See* estates, temple and palace
Terqa, *10*, 82–83
textiles, 13, 24, 35, 64–66, 70–72, 84
Thebes, *8*
Third Dynasty of Ur, 51–62
  documents from, 79
  end of, 61–62
  kings of, 125. *See also* Shulgi; Ur-Namma
  legal system of, 51–52, 55–58
  standardizations in, 52, 55
  taxation and redistribution in, 58–61
  ziggurat construction during, 52–53
Thutmose III (king of Egypt), 87, 126
Tigris River, *8*, *12*, *13*, 61
timber. *See* wood
time measurements. *See* months; year-names, 1
tin, 13, 64, 66–67, 70–72
tokens in accounting, 22
tombs. *See* burials
trade, 14, 42, 63–73
  and Akkadian Empire, 42
  and colonization, 25
  and distribution of natural resources, 13–14
  and international relations, 7
  and Old Assyrian colonies, 63–68
  and Third Dynasty of Ur, 51
trash, 3
treasure hunters, 5
treaties, 46, 64–68, 92–96
  Late Bronze Age Hittite-Egyptian treaty, 92–94
  Old Assyrian trade treaty, 64–68
  peace treaty, 46, 92–96
  trade treaty, 64
tribute, 41, 103
Tummal, 59–60
Turkey (Anatolia), 7
Tushratta (king of Mittani), 88–91, 126

U

Ugarit, 111
Umma, *12*, 35–37, 41
Ur, *8*, *11*. *See also* Third Dynasty of Ur
  and economic documents, 23
  economy of, 43
  god of, 52
  high priestess of, 43
  and hymn of Enheduanna, 45
  kings of, 52, 57, 62
  and Lagash, 36
  royal tombs of, 37–39, 47
  Sargon's conquest of, 41
  ziggurat construction in, 52–53
Urban Revolution, 25–26, 33
Ur-Namma (king of Ur)
  dates of, 125
  leadership of, 51–52, 62, 101
  and legal system, 51–52, 56–58, 79
  public image of, 53, *54*, 57–58
  and standardizations, 55

Uruk, *8*, *11*, 17–20
and Lagash, 36
Sargon's conquest of, 40–41
and Ur, 45
ziggurat construction in, 52
Uruk period, 23–26, 28, 125
Utnapishtim (legendary survivor of the flood), 109–11

V

votive gifts, 31. *See also* offerings to gods

W

wages, 81–82
wardum, 84
warfare, 36–37, 40–41, 48, 51–52, 61, 63, 75, 85–86, 87, 99, 101, 103–4, 122
weights and measures, standardized, 52, 55
witnesses, 56, 81–85, 93
women, 20, 24, 25, 38, 83–85
in Late Bronze Age, 88–89
in Old Babylonian period, 83, 84–85
rights and freedoms of, 1
and royal marriages, 88–89
in the Uruk period, 24
wood, 2–3, 9, 25, 60
wooden writing boards, 108
wool, 13, 25, 66. *See also* textiles
Woolley, Sir Leonard, 37–38
workers. *See* laborers
writing. *See also* cuneiform script
audience of, 33
development of, 16–17, 22–23, 58
and early cities, 16–17
Early Dynastic cuneiform, 32–33
kings' use of, 33, 35–36
uses of, 33, 35, 55, 57, 58, 77–79, 91, 98

Y

Yamhad, 74–75
Yarim-Lim (king of Yamhad), 75, 76
year-names, 68–69, 76–77, 85
years, measurement of, 85

Z

Zagros Mountains, *11*, 51
Zidahri, 59–60
ziggurat construction, 52–53, 77, 113
ziggurats, 77, 113, 117
Zimri-Lim (king of Mari), 74, 75, 125